Reach Your Potential

PISCES

Teresa Moorey

ISBN 0 340 69720 2

First published 1998
Impression number 10 9 8 7 6 5 4 3 2 1
Year   2002   2001   2000   1999 1998

Typeset by Transet Limited, Coventry, England.
Printed in Great Britain for Hodder & Stoughton Educational, a division of
Hodder Headline plc, 338 Euston Road, London NW1 3BH by Cox and Wyman,
Reading, Berks.

Contents

Introduction

A PERSPECTIVE ON ASTROLOGY

Interest in the mystery and significance of the heavens is perhaps as old as humanity. If we can cast our imaginations back, to a time when there were no street lamps, televisions or even books, if we can picture how it must have been to have nothing to do through the deep nights of winter other than to sit and weave stories by the fire at the cave mouth, then we can come close to sensing how important the great dome of stars must have seemed in ancient times.

We are prone to believe that we are wiser today, having progressed beyond old superstitions. We know that all stars are the same as our Sun – giant nuclear reactors. We know that the planets are lumps of rock reflecting sunlight, they are not gods or demons. But how wise are we in truth? Our growing accumulation of facts brings us no closer to discovering the real meaning behind life. It may well be that our cave-dwelling ancestors knew better than us the meaning of 'holism'. The study of astrology may be part of a journey towards a more holistic perception, taking us, as it does, through the fertile, and often uncharted realms of our own personality.

Until the seventeenth century astrology (which searches for the meaning of heavenly patterns) and astronomy (which seeks to clarify facts about the skies) were one, and it was the search for meanings, not facts that inspired the earliest investigations. Lunar phases have been found carved on bone and stone figures from as early as 15,000BCE (Before Common Era). Astrology then evolved through the civilisations of Mesopotamia and Greece, among others.

Through the 'dark ages' much astrological lore was preserved in Islamic countries, but in the fifteenth century astrology grew in popularity. Queen Elizabeth I had her own personal astrologer, John Dee, and such fathers of modern astronomy as Kepler and Galileo served as court astrologers in Europe.

Astrology was taught at the University of Salamanca until 1776. What is rarely appreciated is that some of our greatest scientists, notably Newton and even Einstein, were led to their discoveries by intuition. Newton was a true mystic, and it was the search for meaning – the same motivation that inspired the Palaeolithic observer – that gave rise to some of our most brilliant advances. Indeed Newton is widely believed to have been an astrologer. The astronomer Halley, who discovered the famous comet, is reported to have criticised Newton for this, whereupon Sir Isaac replied 'I have studied it Sir, you have not!'

During the twentieth century astrology enjoyed a revival, and in 1948 The Faculty of Astrological Studies was founded, offering tuition of high quality and an examination system. The great psychologist Carl Jung was a supporter of astrology, and his work has expanded ideas about the mythic connections of the birth chart. Astrology is still eyed askance by many people, and there is no doubt that there is little purely scientific corroboration for astrology – the exception to this is the exhaustive statistical work undertaken by the Gauquelins. Michel Gauquelin was a French statistician whose research shows undeniable connection between professional prominence and the position of planets at birth. Now that the concept of a mechanical universe is being superseded, there is a greater chance that astrology and astronomy will reunite.

Anyone who consults a good astrologer comes away deeply impressed by the insight of the birth chart. Often it is possible to see very deeply into the personality and to be able to throw light on current dilemmas. It is noteworthy that even the most sceptical of people tend to know their Sun sign and the characteristics associated with it.

WHAT IS A BIRTH CHART?

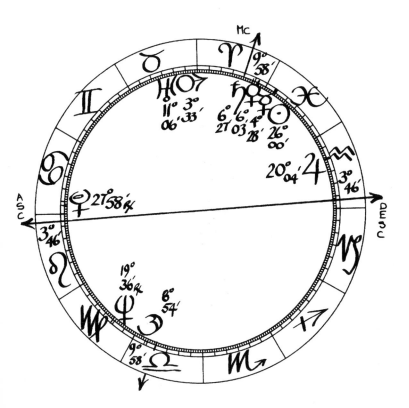

The chart of Rudolph Nureyev
One of the greatest dancers of all time, Nureyev expressed the grace and fluidity of his Pisces Sun in the ballet.

Your birth chart is a map of the heavens drawn up for the time, date and place of your birth. An astrologer will prefer you to be as accurate as you can about the time of day, for that affects the sign rising on the eastern horizon. This 'rising sign' is very important to your personality. However, if you do not know your birth time a chart can still be compiled for you. There will be some details missing, but useful interpretations may still be made. It is far better for the astrologer to know that your birth time is in question than to operate from a position of false certainty. The birth chart for Rudolph Nureyev (page 3), is a simplified chart. Additional factors would be entered on the chart and considered by an astrologer, such as angles (aspects) between the planets, and the houses.

The birth chart shows each of the planets and the Moon in the astrological signs, and can be thought of as an 'energy map' of the different forces operating within the psyche. Thus the Sun sign (often called 'birth sign' or 'star sign') refers only to the position of the Sun. If the planets are in very different signs from the Sun sign, the interpretation will be greatly modified. Thus, if a person has Sun in Leo yet is somewhat introverted or quiet, this may be because the Moon was in reserved Capricorn when that person was born. Nonetheless, the Sun represents the light of consciousness, the integrating force, and most people recognise that they are typical of their Sun sign, although in some people it will be more noticeable than in others. The planets Mercury and Venus are very close to the Sun and often occupy the same sign, so intensifying the Sun-sign influence.

This book is written about your Sun sign, because the Sun sign serves as an accessible starting point for those wishing to learn about themselves through astrology. However, do not let your interest stop there. If you find anything helpful in comments and advice stemming from Sun sign alone, you will find your true birth chart even more revealing. The address of the Faculty of Astrological Studies appears in 'Further Reading' at the back of this book, and it is a good idea to approach them for a list of trained astrologers who can help you. Moon *phase* at birth (as distinct from Moon sign) is also very important. *The Moon and You for Beginners* (see 'Further Reading') explains this fascinating area clearly, and provides a simple chart for you to look up your Moon phase, and learn what this means for your personality.

The **planets** are life principles, energy centres. To enable you to understand the birth chart, here are their glyphs:

Sun	⊙	Jupiter	♃
Moon	☽	Saturn	♄
Mercury	☿	Uranus	♅
Venus	♀	Neptune	♆
Mars	♂	Pluto	♇ (♇)

Rising Sign or **Ascendant** (**ASC**) is the way we have of meeting the world, our outward persona. **Midheaven** (**MC**) refers to our image, aspirations, how we like to be seen.

The **signs** are modes of expression, ways of being. Here are their glyphs:

Aries	♈	Libra	♎
Taurus	♉	Scorpio	♏
Gemini	♊	Sagittarius	♐
Cancer	♋	Capricorn	♑
Leo	♌	Aquarius	♒
Virgo	♍	Pisces	♓

Using knowledge of the glyphs you can see that the Sun is in Pisces in our example birth chart (page 3).

■ HOW DOES ASTROLOGY WORK?

We cannot explain astrology by the usual methods of cause and effect. In fact, there are many things we cannot explain. No one can define exactly what life is. We do not know exactly what electricity is, but we know how to use it. Few of us have any idea how a television set works, but we know how to turn it on. Although we are not able to explain astrology we are still able to use it, as any capable astrologer will demonstrate.

Jung discovered something called 'synchronicity'. This he defined as 'an acausal connecting principle'. Simply, this means that some events have a meaningful connection *other than cause and effect.* The planets do not cause us to do things, but their movements are synchronistic with our lives. The old dictum 'as above, so below' applies here. It is a mystery. We can't explain it, but that doesn't mean we should refuse to believe in it.

The planetary positions in your birth chart are synchronistic with the time of your birth, when you took on separate existence, and they are synchronistic with your individuality in this life.

■ MYTH AND PSYCHOLOGY

The planets are named after the old gods and goddesses of Rome, which in turn link in with Greek and other pantheons. The planets represent 'life principles' – forces that drive the personality, and as such they can be termed 'archetypal'. This means that they are basic ideas, universal within human society and are also relevant in terms of the forces that, in some inexplicable way, inhabit the corners of the universe and inform the Earth and all human institutions. Thus the assertive energy that is represented by Mars means energetic action of all sorts – explosions and fires, wars, fierce debates and personal anger. Put briefly, here are the meanings of the planets:

- Mercury – intellect and communication
- Venus – love, unifying, relating
- Mars – assertion, energy, fighting spirit
- Jupiter – expansion, confidence, optimism
- Saturn – limitation, discipline
- Uranus – rebellion, independence
- Neptune – power to seek the ideal, sense the unseen
- Pluto – power to transform and evolve

These principles are modified according to the astrological sign they inhabit; thus Venus in Pisces may be gently loving, dreamy and self-sacrificing, while Venus in Aries will be demanding and adventurous in relationships. Thus the planets in signs form a complex psychological framework – and that is only part of the story of chart interpretation!

In the old mythologies these 'energies' or 'archetypes' or 'gods' were involved in classical dramas. An example is the story of Saturn and Uranus. Uranus is the rejecting father of Saturn, who later castrates and murders his father – thus innovative people reject reactionaries, who then murder them, so the revolutionary part of the personality is continually 'killed off' by the restrictive part. The exact positions and angles between the planets will indicate how this and other myths may come to life. In addition, the mere placement of planets by sign – and, of course, especially the Sun sign, call forth various myths as illustrations. The ancient myths are good yarns, but they are also inspired and vivid dramatisations of what may be going on repeatedly within your personality and that of your nearest and dearest. Myths are used by many modern psychologists and therapists in a tradition that has grown since Jung. We shall be using mythic themes to illustrate internal dynamics in this book.

■ THE SIGNS OF THE ZODIAC

There are twelve signs, and each of these belongs to an Element – Earth, Fire, Air or Water, and a Quality – Cardinal, Fixed or Mutable. The Cardinal signs are more geared to action, the Fixed tend to remain stable and rooted, whereas the Mutable signs are adaptable, changeable.

SIGN	QUALITY	ELEMENT
Aries	Cardinal	Fire
Taurus	Fixed	Earth
Gemini	Mutable	Air
Cancer	Cardinal	Water
Leo	Fixed	Fire
Virgo	Mutable	Earth
Libra	Cardinal	Air
Scorpio	Fixed	Water
Sagittarius	Mutable	Fire
Capricorn	Cardinal	Earth
Aquarius	Fixed	Air
Pisces	Mutable	Water

Jung defined four functions of consciousness – four different ways of perceiving the world – 'thinking', 'feeling', 'sensation' and 'intuition'. Thinking is the logical, evaluative approach that works in terms of the mind. Feeling is also evaluative, but this time in relation to culture and family needs. This is not the same as emotion, although 'feeling' people often process emotions more smoothly than other types. Jung saw 'feeling' as rational, too. 'Sensation' refers to the 'here and now', the five physical senses, while 'intuition' relates to the possible, to visions and hunches. Jung taught that we tend to have one function uppermost in consciousness, another one or maybe two secondary and another repressed or 'inferior', although we all possess each of these functions to some degree.

Jungian ideas are being refined and expanded, and they are incorporated into modern methods of personality testing, as in the Myers-Briggs test. If a prospective employer has recently given you such a test, it was to establish your talents and potential for the job. However, the basic four-fold division is still extremely useful, and I find it is often of great help in assisting clients to understand themselves, and their partners, in greater depth – for we are all apt to assume that everyone processes information and applies it in the same way as we do. But they don't! It is worthy of mention that the important categories of 'introverted' and 'extraverted' were also identified by Jung. In astrology, Fire and Air signs seem to be extraverted, broadly speaking, and Earth and Water introverted – and this has been borne out by the statistical research of the astrologer, Jeff Mayo. However, this doesn't mean that all feeling and sensation people are introverted and all intuitives and thinkers extraverted – this is definitely not the case, and calls for more detailed examination of the chart (e.g. lots of Fire and Water may mean an extravert feeling type).

Very broadly speaking we may link the Fire signs to intuition, Water to feeling, Earth to sensation and Air to thinking. Often thinking and feeling are drawn together and sensation and intuition are attracted, because they are opposites. This probably happens because we all seek to become more whole, but the process can be painful. The notion of the four functions, when understood, does help to throw light on some of the stumbling blocks we often encounter in relationships. However, some people just do not seem to fit. Also Fire doesn't always correspond to intuition, Water to feeling, etc. – it seems this is usually the case, but not all astrologers agree. Some link Fire with feeling, Water with intuition, and most agree that other chart factors are also important. As with all theories, this can be used to help, expand and clarify, not as a rigid system to impose definitions. We shall be learning more about these matters in relation to the Sun sign in the following pages.

■ THE PRECESSION OF THE EQUINOXES

One criticism often levelled at astrology is that 'the stars have moved' and so the old signs are invalid. There is some truth in this, and it is due to a phenomenon called 'The Precession of the Equinoxes'. The beginning of the sign Aries occurs when the Sun is overhead at the equator, moving northwards. This is called the Spring Equinox, for now day and night are equal all over the globe, and the first point of Aries is called the 'equinoctial point'. Because the Earth not only turns on its axis but 'rocks' on it (imagine a giant knitting needle driven through the poles – the Earth spins on this, but the head of the needle also slowly describes a circle in space) the 'equinoctial point' has moved against the background of stars. Thus, when the Sun is overhead at the equator, entering Aries, it is no longer at the start of the constellation of Aries, where it occurred when the signs were named, but is now in the constellation of Pisces. The 'equinoctial point' is moving backwards into Aquarius, hence the idea of the dawning 'Aquarian age'.

So where does that leave astrology? Exactly in the same place, in actuality. For it all depends on how you think the constellations came to be named in the first place. Did our ancestors simply look up and see the shape of a Ram in the sky? Or did they – being much more intuitive and in tune with their surroundings than we are – feel sharply aware of the quality, the energies around at a certain time of the year, and *then* look skyward, translating what they sensed into a suitable starry symbol? This seems much more likely – and you have only to look at the star groups to see that it takes a fair bit of imagination to equate most of them with the figures they represent! The Precession of the Equinoxes does not affect astrological interpretation, for it is based upon observation and intuition, rather than 'animals in the sky'.

■ USING THIS BOOK

Reach Your Potential – Pisces explores your Sun sign and what this means in terms of your personality; the emphasis is on self-exploration. All the way through, hints are given to help you to begin to understand yourself better, ask questions about yourself and use what you have to maximum effect. This book will show you how to use positive Piscean traits to your best advantage, and how to neutralise negative Piscean traits. Don't forget that by reading it you are consenting, however obliquely, to the notion that you are connected in strange and mysterious ways to the web of the cosmos. What happens within you is part of a meaningful pattern that you can explore and become conscious of, thereby acquiring greater influence on the course of your life. Let this encourage you to ask further questions.

Some famous Pisceans

Jilly Cooper, Vaslav Nijinski, Rudolph Nureyev, George Harrison, Maurice Ravel, Roger Daltrey, Rimsky-Korsakov, Michaelangelo, The Duke of York, Elizabeth Browning, Enrico Caruso, Frederick Chopin, Albert Einstein, Handel, Rex Harrison, Victor Hugo, Ted Kennedy, Auguste Renoir, Dinah Shore, Elizabeth Taylor, George Washington.

Pilchard, piranha, or porpoise – what sort of Pisces are you?

Here is a short quiz to give you an idea of how you are operating at the moment. Its tone is light-hearted, but the intent is serious, and you may discover something interesting about yourself. Don't think too hard about the answers, just pick the one that appeals to you the most.

1. **Someone in your group of friends is very eager to go out with you. Everyone says 'Give it a go' but somehow you just don't feel right about it. What do you do?**

   a) ☐ Go into evasive mode, in a way that ruins your social life and wears out your ansafone machine. You don't really want a confrontation. How long can you keep this up?

   b) ☐ Smile and flirt. You're aware that this person's interest is piquant. When pushed you keep giving 'definite maybes' and finding that you have to wash your hair.

   c) ☐ Say kindly that at the moment you are too busy to get involved. You don't want to hurt him or her, but you're really not interested.

2. **The structure has changed at work and you have a new supervisor who expects more, watches you and criticises. How do you react?**

   a) ☐ Feel nervous and upset. Head for the Prozac.

   b) ☐ Spend a long time in the lavatory and take days off. Mysteriously important papers go missing, but you haven't seen them . . .

   c) ☐ It's time to leave. After all, you've been meaning to get yourself something more creative and offering more freedom.

3. **Your family or group of friends have decided on a holiday some-where you hate – all that heat, flamenco and chips. How are you going to get out of this?**

a) ☐ You go along with the plans. When you are away you are ill for most of the time and someone has to look after you.

b) ☐ You adopt a long-suffering expression. Attractive brochures keep appearing and you drop hints. Then you have one of your migraines (Paris here you come!).

c) ☐ You aren't that bothered as long as everyone's happy and the wine is good. You get in a stock of your favourite novels to read while away.

4. **On an exhausting journey you slump into the last seat on a bus or train. Then an old lady walks in, looking decidedly too doddery for strap-hanging. What do you do?**

a) ☐ You bury your head in your book or magazine.

b) ☐ You sigh and clutch your temples dramatically.

c) ☐ You get up and offer your seat. An interesting chat ensues and at the end of the journey you swap addresses – you have received another indication of life's endless variation and mystery.

5. **You are out shopping with a friend when you are approached by a gypsy selling charms. Your friend scoffs, but you might like to buy one – so what do you do?**

a) ☐ Pretend disinterest and run back and get one while your friend is stuck in a queue.

b) ☐ Say 'Poor old thing, she looks so cold and ragged', buy the charm you want – and you've got no money left, so your mate buys you coffee.

c) ☐ You like the idea of both the charm (which is no doubt a fake) and helping the gypsy. You get out your cash – what does it matter what your friend thinks?

6. **You form a long-term relationship with someone who turns out to have a severe problem with alcohol or drugs. You are deeply attached emotionally, and practically your assets are entwined. What do you do?**

a) ❑ This is probably your fault. You clean up, give support and keep quiet.

b) ❑ You tell the sad tale to all and sundry and weep and rave at your lover. Despite all the advice you get, nothing changes.

c) ❑ You make it your business to learn as much as you can about the addiction, so you can give help based on knowledge, and you seek professional guidance.

7. **A good friend turns up to borrow money for a night out. Despite being a really pleasant companion, this person has a well-deserved reputation for not paying debts, so you:**

a) ❑ Get out your money – how can you refuse?

b) ❑ Get out your purse, regaling him or her with stories of how your mother is sick and you need cash for bus fares to the hospital. Eventually you produce one crumpled note.

c) ❑ You like this person. You work out how much you can afford to lose at the moment and give that and no more.

8. **Your attitude to the occult is:**

a) ❑ Lots of people say there is something in it, so perhaps there is . . .

b) ❑ It doesn't do to argue with people who say they've had experiences, and you've had occasional 'feelings'. Your horoscope once warned of an accident, and that was handy to get you out of making a journey you wanted to avoid.

c) ❑ You've had many 'feelings' and even precognitions. Anything is certainly possible, but you don't believe all you hear.

9. **A challenging, new, creative project is taken on at work, requiring talents that you may well possess but are hitherto untested. How do you deal with this situation?**

a) ☐ Decline the opportunity, saying you are not up to it and you don't want to let anyone down.

b) ☐ You'd probably accept, and hope for the best. If work is turned in late, or shoddy, it would probably be the fault of the computer program or something else.

c) ☐ Accept nervously and excitedly, and start casting around for ideas.

Now count up your score. What do you have most of – a's, b's or c's?

Mostly a's. At the moment you are a bit of a pilchard, aren't you? You don't stand up for yourself, or have the courage of your convictions. You are sensitive to the feelings of others, and yet you become so depleted that you are not able to put this to good use – you conform and shrink from confrontation. What is the worst that can happen if you say 'no'? Maybe you should practise standing up for yourself in small matters at first. It is not that you are simply weak – you have just not learnt to deal with your sensitive, receptive nature. Start being true to yourself, and 'find' yourself.

Mostly b's. You're in piranha mode at the present, and you get your own way by manipulating and getting under people's skin, often by making them feel guilty. You are no stranger to evasion and self-pity. Sometimes you can be quite destructive and even deceitful. You are no doubt clever, subtle and have good instincts – when are you going to put these to work? Stop going at everything by roundabout routes and don't be afraid to use your powers of persuasion openly. Enjoy *using* your empathy and compassion – it's more fulfilling than eliciting it.

Mostly c's. Generally kind and caring, you listen to that 'still, small voice' and follow it, rather than the herd. You have faith in life and you find this is justified by the rewards you get back. Intuitive and empathic, you have an excellent sense of under-currents and while you are generous, you also possess a sense of self-preservation. However, this probably doesn't prevent you from feeling let down by others on occasion. Are you aware that you may make them feel uneasy by being 'too good to be true'? Maybe you could be a little more demanding sometimes. Don't forget to take your share.

If you found that in many cases none of the answers seemed anywhere near to fitting you, then it may be that you are an uncharacteristic Pisces. This may be because there are factors in your astrological chart that frustrate the expression of your Sun sign, or it may be because there is a preponderance of other signs, outweighing the Pisces part. Whatever the case may be, your Sun-sign potential needs to be realised. Perhaps you will find something to help ring a few bells in the following pages.

1 The essential Pisces

I . . . heard a mermaid on a dolphin's back
Uttering such dulcet and harmonious breath
That the rude sea grew civil at her song,
And certain stars shot madly from their spheres
To hear the sea-maid's music

Oberon in *A Midsummer Night's Dream*, Shakespeare

■ MERMAIDS AND MERMEN

No one can understand Pisces, and this fact is often dismissed with a wave of the hand and a 'Well, they don't even understand themselves!' Of course they don't – at least not with the logical mind. Every Pisces worth their sea-salt knows quite well that some things cannot be understood rationally – for example the human heart, the nature of the cosmos and the fluctuations in the price of fish, to take a characteristically Piscean broad sweep. Many Pisceans have a consciousness, an acceptance and an instinct concerning subjects that others dismiss as incomprehensible. Pisces does not have to explain, for Pisces knows. Yes, it is true Pisces can go to extremes. This is the sign of the artist, mystic, priestess or priest, but it also encompasses the pill-swilling alcoholic no-hoper. In between we have bland Pisceans, prosaic Pisceans, conventional Pisceans – and even super-rational and aggressive Pisceans. Pisces is Everyone, and Pisces is Mystery. Others should never assume they know Pisces, for when everything seems at its clearest it is possible that all they are seeing is their own reflection.

■ PISCES BODY LANGUAGE

Many of you Pisceans are extremely graceful, for this sign is associated with dancing. Others have all the deportment of a landed seal. Much depends on how at ease you are with yourself and your surroundings. Yours can be an absent-minded sign, prone to kicking milk bottles and tripping over doormats. However, many of you display a fluidity and ease of movement that derives from a laid-back, tolerant outlook and an instinct for balance and beauty. Like the other Water signs, Pisces is sensitive to the social undercurrents – in fact, Pisces is *the* most sensitive of all signs in this respect. Chameleon-like, you will take on the colour of your surroundings, often talking with the accent of your current companions and instinctively adapting gesture and expression in order to be easily understood and accepted. You often use your hands a lot when talking, and there is often a dreamy look in your eyes as you conjure up the internal images behind what you are saying. Most of all, yours is a responsive sign – others can make you laugh or cry with stories of their triumphs and tragedies. They may find you tend to take up a similar physical position, mirroring their body language. Most people are reassured by this and take you into their confidence, while others are disconcerted. However, it must be remembered that all physical matters are heavily influenced by the Rising Sign, not merely the Sun sign.

■ MYTHS OF THE FISH

One myth concerning the constellation of Pisces tells of how Venus and Cupid were terrified by the monster Typhon, and threw themselves into the Euphrates where they became fishes, and this event was commemorated by elevating the fishes to the sky. However, this tale is probably a corruption of the story of Aphrodite (the Greek counterpart of Venus) rising 'foam-born' from the sea. Many goddess-themes were debased in the Greek and Roman pantheons, and Aphrodite was initially much more than goddess of love and lust. She was initially an Eastern Mediterranean goddess, an ancient and powerful figure of the Creatrix. The fish itself is a primordial symbol of the Goddess, for the oceans were – and are – the cradle of life. Links between the fish and the external female genitalia are often made. In earlier times there was nothing prurient in this, but rather a recognition of the sacred, for the exposed vulva of the Goddess was at once the fountain of life and a source of healing.

The last 2,000 years have been referred to as the Age of Pisces, due to the backward movement of the equinoctial point (see page 10), which is presently entering Aquarius – hence the much vaunted 'Age of Aquarius'. Sadly the 'Age of Pisces' has been far from a tale of enlightenment, but rather a sorry saga of war, fanaticism and destruction. Many people attribute this to the 'dual nature' of Pisces and to the activities of the 'dark fish', that sinister alter-ego that Pisces is said to possess. Of course, we all have a 'dark side' and Pisces is no exception, but Pisces is multiple rather than dual. The Fishes joined by a cord and swimming in opposite directions can be interpreted as a nature torn between the transcendent and the demonic. However, this cord is depicted as an elegant curve, not taut as in a tug-of-war. The Fishes, eyes on either sides of their heads, see many forms, many shifting shapes and symbolise the multidimensional possibilities of water. Our culture has not truly encompassed the meaning of Pisces, and splits light from dark, God from devil, logic from instinct and denigrates one half – hardly a wholistic perception. So the cord is cut and one fish is dead.

The wisdom that transcends opposites is sought by the mystic and is not easy to achieve on a day-to-day level. Many Pisceans shirk the challenge and slide into the nondescript. Others, it is true, do seem in the grip of their own private and monstrous octopus and let all hope of real achievement wither on some far shore while they sail off on their daydreams. However, some Pisceans are inspired. For most Pisceans, the great gifts of the swimming Fishes appear as a simple acceptance of most things, a tolerant viewpoint that does not demand judgement but pours the waters of compassion on all and sundry and a quiet wisdom that does not proselytize but just – is. It's not a cop-out; in fact, this position is barely comfortable. Anyone who calls Pisces 'weak' is simply unaware of the immense strength it takes to look upon the world's pain and to be unable to close one's eyes. No wonder some Pisceans are 'escapist' or simply deny what they see by immersion in the commonplace. More generally, Pisces steers a course of genial compromise. People of extremes? Maybe. However, there may be no hint of the many undercurrents on the smooth, sun-dappled surface. Come on in – the water's lovely!

■ ELEMENT, QUALITY AND RULING PLANET

We have seen that each of the signs of the zodiac belongs to one of the Elements, Earth, Fire, Air or Water, and to one of the Qualities, Cardinal, Fixed or Mutable. Pisces is Mutable Water. This means that Pisces is fluid, malleable and uncontainable. The Element of Water flows in and around, transforming, gestating, fertilising, concealing. Water-sign people are associated in general with emotions, relationships and human values. Pisces is conscious not only of personal emotions, but also of the condition of humanity and the history, and scope of human anguish is a matter of almost personal concern to some Pisceans.

We have seen that the Element of Water has some things in common with what Jung called the Feeling function. Feeling is not about anger, desire, love, rage, spilling out all over the place, but about an evaluative system that prioritises what is of importance in human bonds and sympathies. 'Feeling' people may deal fairly well with emotions, which does not mean they are controlled by their loves and hates, but rather that they are aware of them and work with them, rather than against them. Jung stressed that Feeling was rational. You Pisces people may not be logical, but common sense and instinct usually underpin your actions, and while you may not be able to explain yourself cogently (and may lose confidence in yourself if forced to do so) there is coherence and wisdom in your approach.

Pisceans also often exhibit 'feelings' in another sense of the word, in that you possess an uncanny intuition about what is going on inside the heads of other people and what they are going to do. Feelings of all kinds are given a low priority in a society that exalts scientific detachment, and this often encourages Pisceans to be mute, mysterious, or just to feel misunderstood. While it does no harm for any of the Water signs to strive for a measure of objectivity, Piscean strengths lie in the intuitional and the emotional, and it is vital that this is respected.

Pisces is the twelfth, and last, sign of the zodiac. At the Spring Equinox the astrological year commences with Aries the Pioneer, followed by Taurus the Settler and Farmer, then Gemini the Communicative Thinker. Then comes Cancer, the first Water sign, of the Tribe and Family, followed by Leo the Monarch, and Virgo the Sorter and Reaper. Libra the Diplomat precedes Scorpio, second Water sign of Passion and Transformation. Sagittarius the Philosopher comes next, then Capricorn the Builder, and Aquarius the Revolutionary, bringing us up to date with Pisces, sign of the Mystic and the Poet. The twelve signs represent twelve principal modes of human behaviour, or the structure of human society, separated into twelve strands. Pisces comes last but not least, for in Pisces all is combined and all may be dissolved to make way for a rebirth into new consciousness. Because of this Pisces is the most unpredictable and the most difficult to define of all the signs. This is because Pisces is capable of picking up on almost any area of experience and may display qualities of resolution, stubbornness, assertion, detachment and practicality, as well as the more usual attributes of dreaminess and empathy.

In the Northern Hemisphere, Pisces occurs in late winter/early spring. Hope is present in the first signs of resurgence but vitality is still quite low. The cold of winter has depleted resources and there is a sense of waiting and expectancy, dreaming of spring and summer, reflecting upon what the passing winter has left with us. In the North, Pisces may be the pause, the in-breath before the leap. However, in the Southern Hemisphere, Pisces leads us towards the Autumn Equinox – a time to gather in the harvest and to focus upon matters of an inward nature as the nights grow longer and the tide of life retreats once more.

Each sign is said to have a 'Ruling Planet'. This means that there is a planet that has a special affinity with the sign, whose energies are most at home when expressed in terms of that sign. For centuries the 'old' ruler of Pisces was Jupiter, before the discovery of the extra-Saturnian planets, Uranus, Neptune and Pluto. Jupiter, as King of the Gods expresses the expansive, generous and philosophical side of Pisces. The ruler of Pisces is now taken as Neptune, Monarch of the Sea, unpredictable god of storms, calms and unplumbed depths. However, it is noticeable that we have a 'patriarchal' zodiac with only one planet – Venus – named after a goddess. The nature of Neptune, with its mystery and elusiveness, is much more archetypally 'feminine' and while all such qualities can be evinced equally by men, for eons the sea was Goddess. Neptune, as well as linking Pisces to the source of life and to an infinity of perspectives, also bestows the power to apprehend what is unseen and to inspire ideals in his or her children.

■ BEAM ME UP, SCOTTIE

Pisceans are not always able to don the blinkers of routine and forget about things like fate, suffering, the purpose of life, the plight of orphaned children, neglected animals and the casualties of wars around the globe. Besides, Pisces can see so many different angles, so many different 'realities' that existence is something of a kaleidoscope. 'What is reality?' can be a serious question to Pisces. In addition, Pisceans often have high aspirations and far-flung dreams that range in scope from helping friends and family, through creating an eternal masterpiece, to no less than saving the world. Small wonder that many Pisceans can't cope with the lock on their own front door. 'Stop the world, I want to get off!' is a Piscean *cri de coeur*.

There is a part of your Piscean character that really does believe that you should not have to cope with electricity bills, tax demands and cars that won't start; it seems an outrage to some Pisceans to be confronted by the mundane, and indeed many Fish-people find ordinary things a matter of the utmost perplexity. This can be dealt with in a variety of ways, starting with 'helplessness': for this read 'someone to take all those nasty burdens off my shoulders so I can spread my wings' (or rather, fins).

Another classic Piscean way out – and a much more dangerous one – is escapism through drugs. This trait tends to be greatly exaggerated by many astrologers. Pisceans usually inherit, along with your sensitivity, a resilience and toughness that enable you to cope with what other signs only strenuously ignore. However, general love of life and a wish to relax and encompass all does make the occasional little tipple attractive to many Mer-people – everything looks much more rosy from the right side of a glass of burgundy, and that ideal, beautiful world seems more within reach. Pisceans also 'escape' into dilemmas, crises and dramas, not just because you need to suffer and sacrifice – another urge attributed far too often to Pisces – but because these comparatively trivial matters are a distraction from a more universal 'angst'. In this, Pisces may exhibit something of the 'hysterical personality pattern' (although this is by no means confined to Pisces) where true feelings that may be of an unbearable nature are camouflaged by what might justifiably be called a lot of fuss. One example could be a deep fear of abandonment, resulting from childhood trauma and trawling in a nameless terror in the face of the vastness of creation. Dealing with this by flamboyantly drawing the attention of friends and family to every little pimple or lost penny is one way of escape. A more appropriate route, adopted by sensible Pisceans, is that of self-examination, counselling or the development of a spiritual consciousness.

Pisceans do not need to be told to 'come down to earth', 'get real' or 'snap out of it'. You aren't being unrealistic; in fact, you may be far more realistic than most. It is just that 'reality' for Pisces is not bounded by your job, bank balance and next Tuesday's trip to the supermarket. However, you do need to learn that you are not responsible for everything, and that what you cannot change – i.e. 99.9 per cent of what you apprehend – you must turn away from and accept. You need to seek forms of 'escape' that are creative, such as music, literature and the arts. It is one of the Piscean life-tasks to face the fact that your ideals can only ever become real in an infinitesimal way and that that is better than a life of empty pipe-dreams. And for many Pisceans the ultimate solace is found in some form of spiritual or religious observance.

■ KARMA CHAMELEON

Pisces is possibly the most difficult sign of the zodiac to spot, because you have the art of camouflage perfected. You will adopt the views of your companions, as far as possible – Pisces often finds something acceptable in most approaches – you may dress to 'fit in' and tailor your mannerisms to the company you keep. The mere idea of this makes many people uneasy, and Pisces has been labelled two-faced or gullible because of it. Many Pisceans are bland, commonplace and even vacuous with no trace of poet or mystic visible.

It is undeniable that many Pisceans take the line of least resistance – up to a point. The truth of the matter is that you *genuinely* see things from so many sides and you are not lying, or even compromising, when you manage to agree with vastly differing views. However, there is a point beyond which you will not stretch, and many people, believing they have acquired a comfortable side-kick in Pisces, are surprised to discover a streak of ruthlessness in the Fish that they would never have imagined. When pushed too far you may go to extremes of anger and retaliation, or simply cut off. The lights go out in those strange eyes and it is as if others have ceased to exist. It must be remembered that for all the giving qualities of Pisces, you are a person who can never be owned, for a part of you belongs to your own inner mystery, and to the eternal.

You can be a disconcerting person. It has been said that 'in Pisces you see yourself' and this is undoubtedly true, up to a point. Mer-people pick up on the feelings of others by a type of sonar you must have learnt from the dolphins, and it is often much more important to ensure that others are comfortable, before yourself. Your own emotions you can deal with, and you can make it up to yourself later, but the unhappiness of others weighs upon your soul. Of course, this can make you pure heaven to be with, or it can be uncomfortable, because the sensation that others have that their defences are plate glass to Pisces can make them feel laid bare. In addition, those who secretly don't like themselves are not going to feel exactly great when their personality stares at them from the other side of the room! Because of this some people do not trust Pisces.

Many Pisceans know that they must follow a certain destiny, or 'karma' for they have a sense that their life, however insignificant it may seem, really matters and they are aware that all that they do will be examined in the light of eternity. They walk with one foot in the Otherworld, not able to forget for appreciable periods that we live in the world of illusion. Some, on the other hand, choose to ignore this. The sign of Pisces produces more people who suppress and twist their inner nature than almost any other, because this twelfth and last sign can present a difficult and challenging path. Pressures to conform may be relentless and a despair at ever being understood can set in before the individual has achieved any degree of self-awareness. Because Piscean 'truths' are not cerebral, there may be no words for them. Aquarian futuristic and iconoclastic visions can at least be articulated, while Pisces, who may be just as much of a rebel, is left with poetry, at best, and poetry can be difficult to understand.

■ SERVING, SACRIFICING, SUFFERING . . .

Pisces is often termed the sign of self-undoing, born either to suffer or to serve, or perhaps both, but this is most overrated. Many Pisceans are dynamic, creative, self-motivating and highly effectual. Many have a well-developed sense of their own well-being, and while they might not demand loudly to be granted the best bed in the hotel, like a typical Aries or Leo, in a quieter way they usually secure their own feathery nest. Pisces women, in particular, can exhibit determination and practicality that is quite absent from popular descriptions of Pisces, to the extent that there seems to be more at work here than other chart factors counterbalancing Piscean traits. Perhaps this 'givingness' of Pisces needs unpacking.

Let us take the impulse to 'serve' first. This may sound like self-abasement, but it isn't. Pisces *does* like to serve in the sense that you like to believe that what you are doing is helpful and relevant in a wide context, and you do like to champion the disadvantaged. It is rare for a Piscean to be truly content amassing wealth or achieving self-aggrandisement for their own sake. However, Pisces likes money as much as the next person and basks quite happily in the limelight. In general, you gain most fulfilment from feeling the money you have earned is a recognition of artistic or creative achievement as well as hard cash: money earned from a first painting or accepted magazine article will be worth ten times as much as that gained from the daily grind, and will show you that you are 'plugged in' to something that matters. In addition, while you are capable of buying yourself treats, you do like to see that large sums of money are used in a worthwhile fashion, perhaps on family, friends or charity. However, you will usually see that you are okay first. Pisces will serve the needs of others if they are felt to be paramount, but there is a kernel of pride in Pisces – or perhaps it is not so much pride as a precious and inviolable core that reminds you that you carry a spark of the divine, preventing you from endlessly prostituting your generosity where it is exploited. Yes, Pisces may be more capable than most of giving your last penny to a beggar, but this propensity should not be overstressed. So much for 'serving'.

In respect of 'suffering' it is true that Pisces is almost bound to suffer, either because you are so open to the pain of the world that you can never be entirely at peace, or because you have done so much violence to your inner nature in order to avoid this assault that you can know no real fulfilment. However, the other side of the coin is a huge propensity for pleasure, as in 'Eat, drink and be merry, for tomorrow we die'. With infinity around the corner, what is there left to do but lie back and enjoy yourself? Pisceans are no stranger to luxury, laughter and sensuous enjoyment. However, there are Pisceans who adopt the 'martyr' stance for their own ends, but these are another story . . . .

And so to 'sacrifice'. The popular idea of sacrifice is self-deprivation and self-abnegation – a denial of the pure joys of being human as if to punish oneself: sackcloth, ashes, hair shirts and the adoption of misery and discomfort as a way of life. No thanks! Sacrifice is properly a transformative act – it is not a sacrifice of the self, but a giving up of something for the greater Self, that we do in order to change and grow. At its most sublime this amounts to the transcendent experience sought by mystics; ordinary Pisceans rarely aspire to this. At a lesser level it means that real shifts in the personality can be achieved by not being a slave to the desires of the moment. In another respect sacrifice is common sense, for often something has to be 'sacrificed' in life – free time, comfort, security – in order to achieve a long-term goal which may be anything from commitment to a relationship to the embarkation upon a completely new career. Pisces, often able to take a panoramic view, is quite capable of 'sacrificing' present-day needs for a more worthwhile goal.

Yes, it is true that Pisces may put the comforts of others before their own – but not all the time. You like to serve, but also to be appreciated, and you are not a tribe of masochists who enjoy pain, although you may put up with a great deal for a suitable cause. Often it is hard to discern what the purpose of Pisces may be, for yours is anything but an obvious personality.

■ THE OLD BOOT

We are all familiar with the cartoon of the fisherman striving to land a fat catch that turns out to be an old boot. Sometimes that's Pisces – no glistening Fish, but just an old boot. And that boot isn't merely useless and waterlogged: it's also dangerous, full of poisonous weeds and piranha. No good throwing it back in the water for it will still be there, lurking at the bottom of the lake. A close look at the Piscean old boot reveals self-delusion, waste and a pernicious misuse of power.

Let us take self-delusion first. Most of you Pisceans are aware that you delude yourself from time to time; the only trouble is that the delusion, when it's operating, is like an enchanted sleep with no prince's kiss. You can become so separated from reality – which is, after all, hard and boring – that you achieve almost nothing. Part of the reason for this is that you aren't always quite sure *how* you make a thing real, reality being an awkward concept, and all that. A second reason is fear: 'If I give this my best shot and it doesn't come about then I will be left with nothing – not even my dream.' To be abandoned in this cold world without even a dream is a dreadful prospect to Mer-people. Third, a rather more subtle point, is that if you make a dream come true then part of that dream *is still lost*, for anything brought to life is by definition flawed. The poor Fish is well and truly caught in a net!

Waste is a natural product of self-delusion and many Pisceans waste their time and talent – most of you have a talent of one sort of another – by deluding themselves in some way: 'Tomorrow, next week, next year I'll really sit down and get on with it, things will be different, I'll have more free time, a better relationship,' etc., etc. So runs the litany of the loser. So where do we go from here?

The remedy is easy to supply but may be hard to implement. First, Pisceans who have an unfulfilled dream need to remind themselves of a few phrases, several times a day. A good selection might be: 'Show some faith, there's magic all around', 'Fortune favours the brave' and 'Better to regret what you have done, than what you have not done.' Second, and more difficult, not a day should be allowed to pass without bringing the cherished project a little nearer, whether it is a large-scale plan for starting a new charity or a wish to learn how to work with ceramics. You will need to be stern with yourself about this: it may mean writing a letter or making a phone call, searching out a new piece of information or devoting many hours to detailed planning, but it must be a firm commitment. Third, do not let fear of failure ever stop you – we *all* fail, from time to time, it's how we learn. Yes, it will hurt, but it won't kill you, and when you have recovered you will be better equipped to succeed next time.

Misuse of power is a more subtle matter. Pisceans usually possess emotional power. By this I mean that you are fairly well acquainted with how you are feeling, and though you may sometimes kid yourself for a while that you aren't angry or resentful, because this is at war with the more sympathetic aspects of your nature, you usually come to the knowledge sooner rather than later, and this self-acceptance is a kind of power because it supports self-direction. However, there is another kind of power that comes from knowing exactly how other people are feeling, sometimes much better than they do, and of using it for your own ends. In other words, manipulation. If you are patient enough and perceptive enough you may manipulate others into doing what you want, without the other person having much idea what is happening. In addition, you may use the desires and emotions of others, arousing you to feed your own ego and sense of drama.

This sounds rather like emotional vampirism, and in a way it is. It can be sinister and hard to deal with. Such 'underhand' ways are generally despised – but are they really so contemptible? Feelings, after all, are natural currency to the Water signs, and merely because our culture tends to prize confrontation doesn't mean that other approaches are by definition nefarious. Pisces can be deceptive, it is true, but you may be accused of this unjustly by people who basically do not trust themselves. In its extreme form manipulation can be undeniably poisonous, for it may rob another person of their peace of mind and be destructive; it can also be destructive to you, and you may become almost incapable of articulating what you want and going for it in a direct manner, to the point where you almost lose sight of your goal. There are better ways: subtlety is to be recommended and secrecy may sometimes be desirable, but be clear about what you want, what is right for you and others and keep this always in sight. And keep the 'old boot' landed, high and dry.

The Sealskin

Once upon a time, on the roof of the world, a solitary hunter stopped to rest. He could not believe what he saw, for on the beach danced a group of slender, naked women. The hunter had heard stories about how seals, with their soulful eyes, were once human. There, on the white sand, lay several skins, one for each of the glistening dancers. Filled with yearning, the hunter crept from his hiding place and snatched up one of the skins, buttoning it inside his coat. Then he waited.

The dance was over and with silvery laughter the women retrieved their skins – all except one, the most beautiful of all. When all her companions had disappeared beneath the waves the hunter stepped out into the open.

'I have your skin,' he said. 'Come with me. Be my wife, and after seven years I shall return your skin and you may do as you wish.'

What could the seal-maiden do? She agreed, and went with the hunter to his dwelling, where they lived together happily enough. A son was born to them, and yet there was sorrow in the great eyes of the seal-woman, and her skin cracked and became opaque. At the end of the seven years she begged her husband for her sealskin, but he became angry and would not return it. Her son followed his father and found the skin, unearthed it and brought it to his mother.

His mother seized the skin with delight and, slipping into it, she ran for the shore. But the boy ran after her crying 'Mother, don't leave me

– take me with you!' She hesitated, breathed into his mouth her magic breath and took him with her, beneath the waves.

In this world, too wonderful to describe, the boy learnt many things. However, he could not stay forever, for his destiny lay in the upper world, with his father. So, after a while, his mother brought him back to the shore. Kissing him, she took sorrowful leave.

Every time the boy looked out upon the moonlit tide he could feel his mother's presence. Eventually the boy became a celebrated musician, and his greatest joy was to sit upon the shore, playing his pipes and his drums and watching the seal-people dancing, far out upon the waves.

This story is laced with Piscean metaphor and each of the figures is an aspect of Pisces. The man, yearning for the ethereal beauty of the sea, is Pisces. He dares the unknown to gain his dream, but he reneges on his promise – he keeps the skin. There is no happiness that way, for the inspirations of the inner world, of the sea-kingdom, cannot be commanded and must be relinquished at times. Sadly, Pisces must sometimes surrender what is most dear, for it is a thing of inspiration and enchantment and withers if subject to common daylight. Of course, the seal-woman is Pisces, only at home in the emerald depths yet she must come ashore to dance, to mate and to have her child. Fulfilment comes only through making things real, but it is incomplete. And the child is Pisces – offspring of human and sea-creature, at home neither on land nor in the sea, and yet born from both elements. He heals the rift in his soul by his art, his music, his talent and his gift from Otherworld. Perhaps it is the only way.

■ PRACTICE AND CHANGE ■

- It will help you considerably if you can strive for a measure of objectivity – but this should not override your intuition and your sympathetic capabilities.

- Electricity bills and wet Mondays won't go away, however much you despise them. You need to get in the habit of preparing for such eventualities ahead of time – then the 'real' world won't strangle your creativity.

- As a Pisces you are certain to need some form of 'escape', for an unalleviated diet of the commonplace will make you waste away. Don't feel guilty about your 'escapism', but you must ensure that these 'escapes' are not detrimental to your health, general effectuality and relationships.

- Pisces needs a religion, belief or cause to which to offer allegiance. Think about what you need for inner nourishment – you do not have to explain, justify or evangelise.

- What you cannot change you must accept, and put resolutely from your mind. Turn worry time into doing something time, and forget about the rest.

- Don't give until you have nothing left. What are you trying to prove? Do you *really* want to help, or are you expiating some imaginary guilt?

- You may need to remind yourself where you begin and end and where others begin and end. Your personal boundaries may not be clear. You may feel the pain of others as your own, but it isn't yours. Separate, to be effectual.

- Subtlety and keeping your own counsel is one thing, manipulation is another. Ask yourself, if this is applicable, what you are doing and why?

2 Relationships

Wouldst thou . . .
Learn the secret of the sea?
Only those who brave its danger
Comprehend its mystery

Longfellow, *The Secret of the Sea*

There is something missing in the life of a Pisces who is not in love – if not with a person, then with an ideal, a purpose or a dream. In many ways you live to lose yourself in something greater. If a Merperson cannot wake up in the morning to a sense of wonderment, if there is no rosy glow to soften the edges of traffic jams, bank statements and sinks full of washing-up, then life becomes something of a dustbowl, where nothing blooms. However, Pisces rarely gives way to despair. All things are possible, that is the beauty of it – the sorrow of it may be that few actually materialise.

Pisces is usually aching to find someone to give everything to, and it is sad that so few seem to want it. The truth of the matter may be that few people can match your Piscean emotional intensity, and you may mistake caution for the brush-off. Once the relationship is established, you are quite capable of lifting it to the fantasy level, which doesn't mean that you pretend it is something it isn't (although that can happen) but rather that the whole thing becomes highly charged and mythologised. Of course, you can see the whole of life like that, too, and it certainly makes things more interesting, more alive.

It may seem as if Piscean ideals are rather hard to live up to, but that isn't usually the case. You are a devoted and giving lover, looking for the bliss of total surrender. Passionate, responsive, ecstatic, you are looking for union with the Source, but you are rarely flamboyantly expressive or demanding, and will tolerate a great deal from the lover as long as you are sure you are loved. You will go to great lengths to please, for you feel the pleasure or pain of the loved one as if it were your own. Often you are capable of maintaining the glow of enchantment unilaterally, and all that is required of your partner is that he or she should not shatter the dream. However, it is also possible for you to wake up one day and find you have been in love with a mirage. The idol has fallen from her or his pedestal and crumbled to sand. That is the saddest scenario, for nothing ever really existed in the first place.

Pisces will give endlessly of their resources to nurture a partner and many a Pisces has spent years with a no-hoper, caring, believing, supporting, healing. To know you are important to your beloved is reward enough. Other Pisceans, if disappointed, will certainly stray and deceive. You cannot be caged – that would court inevitable disaster sooner or later, for romance dies in a stagnant pool. A little jealousy followed by passionate making-up is romantic, being badgered and confined isn't – unless it's followed by the Great Escape. You need trust and loyalty in order that you can find faith in yourself. If you are accused too long and too often of infidelity, you will probably oblige!

However devoted Pisces may be there is a part of yourself that you always hold back, because it is simply not on offer. This is the secret pact Pisces has with the cosmos, and it isn't negotiable. Others may hurt you, let you down, trample on your illusions, make demands and even abuse you. You may take it all, or you may one day be strangely and permanently absent. You can never be sure, except of one thing – others can never own Pisces. You may give your heart, and your life but you will not give your soul. You have your own moral code that may bear little relationship to anything conventional – so others should not make assumptions. You may be technically faithful for a lifetime, but there is an amoral kernel to Pisces and your dreams will wander where you lust. Even when it seems you cannot possibly be holding anything back, deep inside you are still a law unto yourself – perhaps that is what gives you your strength.

■ PISCEAN SEXUALITY

With all this fantasy floating around one might be forgiven for doubting that Pisces ever descends to something as physical and profane as sex. Of course, there are the occasional Pisceans who do turn to ice when the satin slips back and the candle-glow falls on bare flesh, but it is much more likely that Pisces is erotically and sensually abandoned. Pisces wants to be utterly overwhelmed by the experience of sexual passion. If you are in love, you make love with your soul.

Of course, if Pisces is not in love it may be another story of disgust and cold shoulders, or a subtle and complex power-play. Rarely will you enjoy sex for the physical sensation alone – you aren't quite sure what it means. After all, isn't this whole thing a matter for the emotions, the heart? It is beautiful when love really is involved, but it can be confusing when it isn't and the confusion is compounded because you find it hard to say 'No'. You can maintain a 'definite maybe' for a long time and are quite capable of enjoying the power you have to arouse the other person, while still not wishing to 'hurt his or her feelings'. Pisceans are often chiefly aroused by the arousal of the other party and this can be an immense physical turn-on even where there is almost no other feeling involved. This can be beyond the imagination of many people, and does give rise to hopelessly complex scenarios, where there are multiple dangers and the possibility of great pain for both parties. This is the less acceptable side of Piscean responsiveness and tenderness.

We cannot get way from fantasy, with Pisceans, and it is often in fantasy that Pisces finds the greatest stimulation. Even when you truly love and 'fancy your lover rotten', you will often still find it hard to recapture in the true encounter, the rapture of your imagination. Partners of Pisces do well to remember this, and to supply all the clichés – wine, candlelight, roses and words of love – in order for Pisces to retrieve the ambience. No one can recreate the Piscean dreamscape; that is not required. What will help is for you to be given the opportunity to do so yourself. And erotica: many Pisceans, both male and female, respond to erotica, and some can be very kinky. However, Pisces isn't predictable in this and what appeals one day or to one person may not appeal in another situation. The difference between a turn-on and a turn-off may be almost indistinguishable.

Mr Pisces will almost magic his lover into bed with him by dreaming, imagining and weaving a subtle spell so that the lad somehow finds herself in his arms. He is rarely rough or assertive, but may be so if his lover appears to want that. To call his lovemaking an artform is too cerebral; it is more like a narcotic, slowly and skilfully injected, enhanced by word, deed and symbolism until it is almost harrowingly ecstatic. His taste is for a slow build-up to splendour, rather than meaty grappling, and some Piscean men are only too happy to take a somewhat passive role, with 'girls on top'. Playacting often appeals to Mr Pisces, and he may try almost anything twice. He is more capable of separating sex from love than his female counterpart, or may be conveniently in love for a night, or an hour or two. Emotional content is not as essential to him as to Ms Pisces, but his imagination is a major erogenous zone. He can be quickly and avidly aroused by the correct stimulus but he is also capable of turning into a 'cold Fish' almost unaccountably. However, in general he is tenderness personified, and while in many spheres of life he can be diffident and fearful of making a fool of himself, he knows he can rely on his superb attunement to his lover's responses.

Ms Pisces is seductive, sensuous and giving. She will do almost anything as long as she is made to feel like Helen of Troy, and she can bring out the stud in most men by loving responsiveness. Her lovers shouldn't bother with the leather jockstrap – she will have to use all her self-control not to giggle, and so won't be able to loosen up and make love with the abandonment and dedication she prefers. To her, the greatest turn-on is expression of feeling, but since most men are not particularly good at this, Ms Pisces often feels that she could have been taken higher – she could. The sky isn't the limit; sex can be an interstellar extravaganza for this woman or it can be a disappointment. Like Mr Pisces she can also be strangely detached at times and quite incapable of true response. She may fake it, but more likely she'll gaze off into space and avoid touching. There are the occasional frigid Pisceans, but in the majority of Piscean females the sex drive is high. You may need to be inventive and attentive to coax her back and light her fire, but it will be worth it.

Orpheus in the Underworld

Greek myth tells of Prince Orpheus, who was a hero, a musician and a lover. When his wife Eurydice was bitten by a snake and died, Orpheus could not bear to be without her, so he braved the greatest perils of all – those of the Underworld kingdom – in order to win her back. After many terrible ordeals he stood before the onyx thrones of Queen Persephone and Lord Pluto. There, in the shadows, surrounded by fiends, he played his heartrending music so that the dark queen relented and Pluto motioned that Eurydice be released. 'Look not behind you, minstrel, until you reach the light,' came the terrible whisper of the god of death, 'lest you lose all that which you have gained. Now, begone. Your lover shall follow.'

Joyfully Orpheus set out for the daylight but, as he climbed, his doubts also mounted and he began to wonder if her had been tricked. Perhaps those soft footfalls behind him were those of a fearful monster, and not his darling Eurydice. He willed himself not to look, but just as the first shaft of sunlight fell upon his foot his resolve weakened. Surely it would be all right to take a peep now? He turned, to glimpse his beloved, to touch her hand momentarily before she was sucked back with a shriek into the depths.

Alas, at the last moment, he had lost all he had striven for. Stricken, he leant his back against a tree and pulled disconsolately at the strings of his lyre. Some say he wasted away as he sat, others that he was torn to pieces by a band of wild revellers to whom he did not respond. Tragically, he was reunited with Eurydice in death.

Here we have a story that tells us much about Piscean loves and losses. The prince who charms even the king and queen of the Underworld with his music is Piscean – Pisces can coax beauty from the depths. But the love that seems just within grasp and then fades is also a Piscean theme, not through literal loss but because that hard-won dream seems somehow to evaporate just as it is about to become real. Orpheus renounces life in the way that many Pisceans do, to be united with love in some form. The sheer pathos of the 'so near yet so far' situation is no stranger to Pisces, who may be able to see all too well how things could be, but yet they slide from the Piscean grasp, as phantoms always do. This is not an instruction to Pisces never to try to make things real, but it is a reminder that some things do not belong in this life and a way has to be found to live without them.

■ PISCES WOMAN IN LOVE

This woman has the reputation for being the most ethereally feminine in the zodiac, and while Mermaids do come in all shapes and sizes, the yielding, accepting and slightly helpless quality that Ms Pisces often exudes does tend to make many men feel like Tarzan. Yes, Ms Pisces is capable of devoted hero-worship and can turn her partner into a demi-god. In addition, she rarely blames him when things go wrong, unless she has been badly let down, and the scales really do fall from her eyes. Rarely is she a belligerent feminist – she will love to have doors opened for her or to be carried over the threshold in the tradition of true romance. However, those who think they can do what they like with Pisces had better think again. She doesn't mind playing the little woman because she knows quite well that she can outmatch just about anyone for resourcefulness and sound instinct. She doesn't have to prove she's 'equal'.

One minute Ms Pisces is fluffy slippers and firesides, next minute she's all satin basques and scarlet lips, with several thousand other roles to play in between. She's a child and a witch, a power-dressed career woman, a *Hausfrau*, a seductress and a best mate. You might be forgiven for saying 'Will the real Ms Pisces now please stand up,' but don't bother – she already has, many, many times. She needs a partner badly and there may be a pale and sad aura to the lonely Pisces, which often means some Lothario comes to the rescue and she isn't lonely for long. Men often feel protective towards her and may also assume that they can mould her to their requirements, but although she's nothing if not accommodating she's her own woman underneath.

This woman often finds that she is abused in relationships. She seeks herself in the man she loves, and it may take many years for her to realise that is not where it's at. She can be manipulated by the needs of others (although she can do her own share of manipulating, also) and she can be shattered by infidelity. However, she isn't given to jealous suspicion, because she somehow 'knows' how her partner feels. If he has fallen out of love with her, she is bereft. If things go wrong Ms Pisces often blames herself, sometimes for a long time.

Ms Pisces may consider the 'world well lost for love', but she sometimes realises that her 'world' has been mortgaged to an illusion. Never mind, this woman is the last of the great romantics, and she will never quite give up the dream of how love could be. After all, if she can imagine it, then somehow, somewhere it must be real. She will do practically anything for the man she loves – but she needs a creative outlet and a life of her own. Her partner should encourage her and support her, and let her do the same for him. He shouldn't patronise her or disregard her dreams, or expect her to be exactly the same, say and do the same thing day after day, week after week, because she just can't. She belongs to Otherworld, but she is present in this one for moments – and moments turn into days, days turn into years.

■ PISCES MAN IN LOVE

Given the Piscean traits of sensitivity and deep feeling, Mr Pisces should be at home with his emotional nature, his needs, loves and fears, able to express this openly and warmly, to give of himself because he has the assurance of knowing and facing his inner nature; he should be supportive and accepting, empathic, assertive, caring, wise and profound. Of course, Mermen can be like that. But the unfortunate truth is that Mr Pisces is often as afraid of his feelings as the next male, and while he may usually (but not always) have some idea how he really feels, he won't let on. This guy may be the best in the zodiac at playing the New Man, but he can use this to keep him from situations where he is committed, pinned down, faced with real intimacy and called upon to express his feelings.

Does this mean that this man is best avoided, for the slippery Fish he is? Pisces is an emotional sign, but the male psyche being what it is, men are usually able to dissociate themselves from how they feel. Mermen don't take well to the macho image, and while they may adopt that as one of their disguises they are just as likely to play anti-hero. Many Pisces men can be super-rational, totally scornful of anything unproven, woolly or even imaginative – which is sad, indeed, for Pisces who tends to base his life on his dreams. However, this guy probably cries buckets at weepy films. If the Pisces boy has been badly bruised, as a man he may appear aloof, sarcastic and cruel, stamping on the sensitive points of others as his own feelings have been trampled. In some ways this is the most difficult sign for a male, for Pisces lacks even the shell of Mr Cancer or the fixity of Mr Scorpio – although he may match Scorpio's intensity and even the vindictiveness on occasion. Often the Merman runs from his feelings, or takes them out on others. However, the Pisces man who, through support, encouragement and understanding manages to embrace the depth and variation of feeling that is his gift, truly is the mature and responsive mate of every girl's dreams.

Mr Pisces is every bit as idealistic as his female counterpart and sees his woman as a goddess. If he has warmth and common sense, then the relationship will survive any hard landings, and he will also be able to give his heart, with exquisite tenderness to a real woman. This man has the soul of a troubadour – he's a poet, a magician, a visionary and a gipsy, *en route* for Lucky Town. His sense of magic and almost worship in love should always be nurtured. Give him his hyacinths for the soul and don't expect him to sort out the bills and pay the mortgage with the reliability of a Capricorn or Taurus. You wanted the Moon, and so you must put up with some moonshine. Mr Pisces can't be always reliable – it has to be said that some can be promiscuous and easily seduced – but if you make him feel good, make him feel he is valued and capable, he is sure to come up trumps. Mates of Pisces should not make the mistake of coping with everything and making like Amazons or viragos. He will take it all, in all probability, and come to hate himself and his partner. The trick with Mr Pisces is to make him feel strong and confident, then he will go from strength to strength, surprising and delighting both himself and you by his capability.

It may sound paradoxical, but it is best to accept that a) his moral code resembles a corkscrew more than the 'straight and true', and b) he needs his mate's utter trust. He will thrive on her love and good opinion and will work his fingers to the bone to make her dreams come true. As long as she believes in him, he can believe in himself, and then he's capable of walking on water. Partners of Pisces need to tread a fine line between support which is essential, and control which is destructive. She shouldn't try to make him into what she thinks he should be, but encourage him to find his own primrose path, and then he can lead her into a Wonderland where money-trees grow. This man can take her on a magic carpet ride or pull the rug out from under her. Mr Pisces should be chosen with care and nurtured.

▓ GAY PISCES

Of all the signs Pisces is surely the most tolerant. Occasionally the more vacuous representatives of the sign do soak up popular opinions like a sponge and may ooze a little judgement here, a little prejudice there. However, it is more characteristic for the Mer-person to smile benignly on 'all acts of love and pleasure' for these strike Pisces as an expression of the best of humanity and far, far better than unkindness and aggression. 'Make love, not war' is the Piscean slogan, whether it's love between man and woman, man and man, woman and woman. Some astrologers assert that Pisces and Aquarius are the two most likely of all the signs to consider relationships with members of their own sex. This sign is not con-cerned with boundaries and can be a real gender-bender. While Aquarius may take pleasure in breaching boundaries, Pisces just ignores them. Pisceans are unlikely to tell themselves that they can-not have sex with someone because he or she is a member of the same sex. To Pisces, it's the spark of the divine in each that counts, and its there in all persons, regardless of gender.

■ PISCES LOVE TRAPS

The mirage

When the heart's on fire, beautiful visions shimmer in the haze of passion. The state of being 'in love' is almost by definition an illuso-ry one. Sooner or later we all come back to bad moods and wet washing, and the ordinary, petty humanity of the god or goddess with whom we fell in love. That doesn't spell disaster, it needs read-justment, and mostly this can be accomplished without too much pain. However, if the person one loved never even existed, then the problem is much worse.

One of the drawbacks of your Piscean idealism and romanticism is that you can fall in love, truly, madly, deeply – with a pure figment of your imagination. Sometimes it takes years for realisation to dawn, and when it does it feels like a tragedy. Strength is revealed as weakness, intelligence as foolishness, reliability as deception. Half a lifetime may have been wasted before Pisces wakes to a grey dawn and realises the face on the opposite pillow is that of a stranger. Pisces may not be able to love or even like him or her, and in so doing Pisces despises him or herself for foolishness, continuing forlorn hopes and the dependence on a person Pisces may not even respect. Matters are made worse by the fact that Pisces can feel sorry for and quite unable to hurt the other party, or to loosen their grip on the decaying body of the partnership. This is when Pisces, too, starts to decompose, admitting defeat and floating downstream.

If you find yourself in this dilemma there is no way around it but to face what has happened. Yes, you were wrong. Yes, it's sad. Now, are you really going to sacrifice the rest of your life on the altar of this self-deception? If you are, you have respect neither for yourself nor the other person. There can be a strange egotism in Pisces that believes you are the one-and-only person that can be 'right' for the partner you no longer want – but if it was all so wrong then it's time to move on. Dependency issues can be a problem, but you will need to marshall your faith in life and the basic generosity of the universe. You can't live without a dream, so be realistic! Don't tie yourself to a nightmare.

Slave to love

In love Pisces does tend to give too much. Yours is an excessive sign, immolating itself at the shrine of the beloved. Love and desire turns you inside out, pricked raw by one unthinking word, holding your hands out for the manacles of passion. The underlying truth here is that Pisces is a slave to the essence of love, but not really to the lover. What you want is that your loved one, too, offers him or herself up to this heavenly bondage. All too often, the oblation is unilateral and you are hurt, abused and let down by a partner who can't or won't match the intensity. Hence the Piscean reputation of self-sacrifice, masochism and other forms of abasement. You may throw good love after bad in the belief that sooner or later your loved one will feel the same. When this doesn't happen you may blame yourself, thinking it is because of your shortcomings. But it isn't that at all: most people can't live up to your ideals.

The sublime, the transcendent are there, but they are *in you*. Start thinking about relationships in terms if human values, such as reliability, shared resources, good sex and companionship, and seek the divine somewhere else.

■ PISCES AND MARRIAGE

Pisceans may have an ambivalent attitude to matrimony. On the one hand the idea of 'one man, one wife, one love through life' appeals to your sense of romance and your longing for security. On the other hand you know it usually spells death to glamour and excitement. Some Pisceans resolve this by using the marriage for safety and getting their kicks elsewhere. Some are as slippery as eels and never quite get pinned down. Others slide readily into soft focus and glide down the aisle only to be brought up with a bump by mortgages and commitments.

Those contemplating a contract with a Pisces must try to understand their attitude to marriage before taking the plunge. Pisces may be prone, when confronted by promises 'till death us do part' to ask 'What do you mean by death? Isn't the death of love, the death of hope, a real "death"?' Pisces loves to give all, and marriage is the best theatre for this. Pisceans, on the whole, make devoted partners. You often put the comfort of your mate before your own and you are dedicated to keeping some of that rosy glow wafting over bed and board.

However, this is one marriage where three isn't a crowd – those who marry Pisces don't just marry the person, they marry Piscean dreams.

■ WHEN LOVE WALKS OUT – HOW PISCES COPES

The end of a romance is often a mega-tragedy to Pisces, and it may be impossible to keep this in proportion. Pisces is capable of saying 'You mean everything to me' and really meaning it. So the ending of love can be more like an Apocalypse. Of course, there are Pisceans who may tell themselves they 'didn't really care', or convince themselves that their lover will soon come to her or his senses and come back. It is more usual for Pisces to mourn excessively.

If this has happened to you, the main thing for you and your friends to remember at this point is that *it will not last.* However convinced you may be that this is the 'one and only', no one could ever be that wonderful/perfect/lovable again, this impression will fade with surprising – almost unbelievable – rapidity. Pisces is a fluid, Mutable sign and nothing is more certain than change. Meanwhile, you should be encouraged to talk, cry and even wallow. Friends should give as much support as they can – the impression that your Piscean neediness is just being compounded by sympathy is not usually accurate. Sympathy – or empathy – is really helpful to you. Forlorn Pisceans need to be helped to feel that they are worthwhile, because some sense of identity will have gone out of the window with the lover. More detached souls may find the intensity of Piscean sorrow alarming and may try to shake you out of it, but this is usually a mistake; the more completely all emotion can be felt at the outset, the quicker sorrow will burn itself out. After a while, of course, it may be time for a review. Are you making a habit out of self-pity or at playing the martyr? If so, you need a cause, a creative project or a new love to bring you back to life.

Starting afresh

Despite the extravagance of Piscean grief, it can be amazing to all and sundry how quickly a new love can eclipse the old. Bouncing back like a rubber ball isn't always to be recommended, for you are likely to land slap bang in the middle of something more confusing, illusory and liable to end in disaster than the earlier romance. Pisces people can be very dependent, lacking in confidence, and this applies equally to male and female Pisceans, although males will conceal such traits behind a casual veneer. You can actually manage very well on your own and can find meaning and excitement in single life, but you do need to give yourself a chance to find this. The route to this may be painful and lonely, but if you have established yourself more or less comfortably in a solitary condition you are far better equipped to form a workable relationship.

■ PRACTICE AND CHANGE ■

- Love in some form is probably the most important thing in life to you. For this reason, don't throw it away. Find support from friends, family and groups in order to prevent launching yourself into a relationship for companionship and self-validation.

- Your dreams are your own, but no one can embody them. Do not forget that common sense and day-to-day living are as much the stuff of a successful relationship as romance. Respect and friendship are more important than excitement and drama.

- Try not to expect your partners to be as emotionally attuned and responsive as you are.

- Pisceans often have low self-esteem. Be aware of this and don't let it inveigle you into settling for second best.

- It isn't easy for you to say 'no' but you must find a way, or you will find yourself entrapped over and over again. If you can't say 'no' say nothing, and play for time and space. When you are alone and quiet sort out what you really want and find a way to get it.

- If things go wrong don't blame yourself. Chances are it's at least 50/50. Don't consent to play the 'villain of the piece'.

- Always have an outlet for your creativity, or the danger is that you will put too much into relationships or expect too much from them.

- Learn to stand alone. Often this isn't easy. Once you have learnt that the universe is there for you to explore, you are in a much better position to form a sensible relationship where you do not expect too much.

3 ♓ All in the family

Of the thousands, maybe even millions, of risks we can take in a lifetime the greatest is the risk of growing up

M. Scott Peck, *The Road Less Travelled*

A Pisces in the family is usually a supportive, cohesive influence on the rest of the group. Pisceans are very attuned to family undercurrents and will usually attempt to play the part that ensures the greatest comfort for everyone concerned. They like to heal breaches and pour oil on troubled waters. The risk to them is a loss of their own identity, and all Pisceans need time alone to regenerate and rediscover themselves.

■ PISCES MOTHER

Pisces mothers often do bear out much of the 'suffering' reputation of their sign, because they are so exquisitely and painfully attuned to the pleasures and losses of their offspring and endure all the wounds of childhood over again with each of their children. Sometimes Pisces mother will do almost anything to shield her children, and she really needs to remind herself constantly that no one ever grew up without being hurt; she must not add to her children's burdens by loading them with her worries as well. Pisces mum needs to hold on to her own identity – her children's troubles are their own, *not* hers, and while she may do her utmost to help, in the end the best she can do is to have happiness, fulfilment, and a life of her own; it is probably a mistake for her to give up her career to look after her children.

Pisces mother is typically an easy-going person, and while she may lose her temper in a big way on occasion, she usually gets over it. It is not unknown for Pisces to hold a grudge, but an apology usually ensures that all is forgiven and forgotten. Some Pisceans, because they have chosen to live not for themselves but for their children, can be controlling and manipulative, setting limits that are most 'un-Piscean' in their rigidity and having convenient 'migraines' or stomach upsets whenever it looks as if things aren't going their way.

Pisces mother is not usually good at discipline, and efforts may need to be made to construct a reasonable life structure for the benefit of the family. Here the adaptability of the sign comes into its own, and because Pisces is often able to take a broad and detached viewpoint, important things are given prime attention and details are not fussed about. Pisceans are real 'home makers' with beauty, comfort and ambience having equal attention. Of course, there are also neurotic examples of the sign who do need to have the furniture vacuumed every morning. This sort of Pisces mother is one who has amputated her creative side in favour of domesticity. Both she and her children will suffer unless some outlet for the poetess, seeress, teacher or healer within finds expression.

Pisces isn't very reliable about meals, and may suddenly remember, at 5 p.m. that she hasn't got the ingredients for a meal. However, many Pisces ladies do exhibit a practical streak, and there is an awareness of the necessities of life. Supper might not arrive until 8 p.m., but it will probably be nutritionally balanced or imaginatively produced.

This woman can organise magical birthday parties. At Christmas she gets as excited as the children. If they are ill she can't sleep at night for worrying. She is a great dreamer, and never more so than concerning her children's future. She is especially likely to encourage any artistic talent they may display and is always there in the front row at the school play. Her children may have to learn when to tell her – kindly – that she needs to back off, because she is embarrassing them, and the acid test of whether they experience her as genuinely caring, or controlling and invasive, may come at adolescence. If the teenager can say 'No, Mum, I want to go into town by myself' or 'Mum, please don't cheer for me at sports day', then it means that Pisces mum has in some way succeeded in making the child feel truly cared for, and that the unspoken agenda has not been her need to be needed.

Pisces mum may be ambitious for her children, but what she really wants is for them to be happy. A Pisces mother who is true to her sign and who has not 'sold out' to cultural standards, will be content with any route her children take in life as long as it brings them fulfilment. She is easy to please – and easy to upset. When her children say they're sorry, she will melt.

■ PISCES FATHER

Pisces father can be one of the most loving and sensitive in the zodiac or he may be a rolling stone whose whereabouts and even identity are a mystery. On the other hand, Pisces father can be the ultimate 'New Man' – caring, helpful and supportive. Pisces father can be protective towards his children, although he rarely worries as much as his female counterpart. He may be the most tolerant and easy going of guys when it comes to his own interests, but is all too aware of the unpleasant side of human nature and how it may affect his little ones, and he will do his best to instil his own wisdom into them, by using allegory and fantasy, if necessary. The one thing that may provoke this man, even to violence on occasion, may be a threat to the well-being of his children.

Pisces father is unlikely to want to talk his children out of their dreams and into the family business. He is more likely to teach them to be gentle with worms and flies and to go hunting fairies with them, at the bottom of the garden in the dusk. Of all the males in the zodiac he is the most likely to take to the role of 'house husband'. This man isn't a great one for discipline. However, he usually elicits co-operation because he is prepared to listen and appreciate. Pisces dad doesn't patronise or belittle and he is poignantly aware of the sacred trust of being a father.

This is rarely the 'traditional' father who makes like a stern disciplinarian. However, some Pisceans may sacrifice their individuality to convention, and such a Pisces may be a martinet, with little depth, emotionally inaccessible to wife and family. Other Pisceans may be absent-minded and shambolic, fumbling around in study or potting shed and not affording anything in the way of role model to their children. At their best, however, Pisceans can offer something that, even in this 'New Age' is still rare – a man who is both at ease with his masculinity and able to be sensitive and receptive, who can encourage the individuality of others because he is a free spirit and who looks at the world through eyes that are at once youthful and wise. Pisces father may need to remind himself of boundaries – or his partner will, as everyone comes tumbling in covered in mud with brambles in their hair! He is not good at saying 'No' and may need to realise that his children are going to have to adjust to opposition in life. His task is to show them reality as well as enchantment, although he has a way of making this seem like one and the same thing!

■ THE PISCES CHILD

This dreamy-eyed cherub may be the model son or daughter at times, but at others, may be plain incomprehensible. However, Pisces rarely enjoys being 'a horror' or putting the cat among the pigeons for a bit of fun. Pisces is really difficult only when badly misunderstood or frustrated.

It is important for this young person to be given as much space as possible, mentally and emotionally, while at the same time given maximum support and encouragement. Pisces is an impressionable sign and never more so than during childhood. Sweet, biddable and dreamy, Pisceans need to be able to withdraw regularly to a world of their own that may be inhabited by imaginary playmates. They should never be crushed or patronised. Pragmatic parents may fear that their Pisces children will never 'come good', and that is a sure way to ensure they don't! Pisceans have plenty of common sense and can find their own way of adapting. Their dreams and fantasies will lead them, if they are undisturbed, into ways of coping, not escaping, and they may have some real talent. It is too easy to distort Pisces by pressure to conform. Pisceans are so sensitive to the wishes of their parents that they will play the little intellectual, or the practical one, if they feel that is required, and they will do it convincingly. It is so important not to shape this child according to one's own expectations, for this will take its toll later in life when Pisces becomes a 'lost' soul, or frustrated, confused and escapist. These children need to be encouraged to develop their own identity, which is likely to be rare and whimsical.

Down-to-earth parents may be uneasy at how to handle the Pisceans character, but if so they need to look to themselves for reform, not to Pisces. Parents need not fear, for Pisces also has a healthy sense of self-preservation and will get by just fine. Pisces should not be penalised for 'telling fibs' unless there has been some real harm done to something or someone. The truth of the matter is that Pisces is more likely than most to own up when necessary, for fear someone else might get the blame. At others, Pisces does have a problem with 'reality' and while the Pisces child does need to be helped to cultivate an awareness of the way 'most people' look at things, this should not demolish the 'alternative' reality that is often natural to Pisces. If a dialogue can be set up between these forms of perception it can result in real genius.

Pisceans have antennae for the emotions of others and will do their best to be that which will please, or will heal family rifts. It is better to be quite honest with this Water sign, for if there is trouble between the parents, Pisces will sense this and be much more disturbed than if the matter were out in the open, and discussed. Rigid routines should not be imposed; insist only on that which is essential, and explain why. Pisces is capable of rebellion, sabotage and evasiveness, and if pushed and badgered can turn into the most difficult of children, with all subtlety used to the worst possible ends.

Adolescence is often hard for Pisces children because it may shatter all their dreams, at least temporarily. Now is when Pisces adolescents need lots of encouragement to build up their faith in themselves and their own powers to recuperate and cope, because they can do this resourcefully.

Sex and romance will be important to Pisces and parents shouldn't be too worried about troughs of despair because these are inevitable, and will probably be transitory. However, all Pisces young people need to be talked to in an atmosphere of understanding about how to choose companions and keep undesirable influences at bay. It isn't that Pisceans don't have an instinct for the 'bad guys' because they do. They need to be taught to trust their instincts and to avoid situations where they will be pressurised. Pisces is similar to other children, in that they will feel more able to say 'no' and insist on what they feel is right if they have not had all sense of their own strength and wisdom dinned out of them by adults who insisted they 'knew best' exactly when Pisces should go to bed, what to eat, what to wear. However, being more sensitive than most, Pisces children may become more estranged from their own knowledge of what is right for them if they have been subject to too much coercion, or they may gravitate towards danger 'just for the hell of it'. As in all matters, self-respect is the most important factor. If they have been respected, they will trust themselves.

■ PISCES AS SIBLINGS

It is highly likely that Pisces brothers or sisters will respond in kind to their siblings' treatment of them. It must be admitted that there can be a cruel streak in Pisceans that can emerge if they feel abused, and then they can be cunning, imaginative and resourceful about retaliating. However, Pisceans are often intensely protective towards family members, especially younger ones, and while they might hesitate to battle for themselves they will become savage and fight tooth and claw for someone smaller. Some Pisces siblings may seem a bit 'cut off' and it could be hard to get into their world.

■ PISCES IN THE HOME

Young Pisceans are usually far more concerned with the emotional climate of the home and won't mind too much if there isn't much physical space, as long as there is emotional space and acceptance. However, Pisceans do need some physical space, because they require privacy and time on their own to recharge their batteries. They may be happy with a little nook behind the shed or under the hedge. Contrary to popular reputation, Pisceans are usually fairly tidy. They will need a window to watch the clouds through and murals on the wall will add depth and imaginative stimulation. Obviously a room of one's own is always desirable, but Pisces may become lonely and sometimes fearful of nameless 'things'. Specific instructions may not be appropriate – Pisceans need an adaptable environment where they are 'held' but not confined. In particular, they will love a loft-conversion or a window-seat that is their 'own'. Their privacy should never be invaded.

■ PRACTICE AND CHANGE ■

● Pisces mum must have a life and an occupation of her own – she should be careful not to live through her children for that will be burdensome for the child.

● In the home, all Pisceans need time alone and that should be respected. Many Pisces will like to have a special 'place'.

● Pisces parents must beware of controlling and manipulating their children by a type of moral blackmail.

● Pisces parents must preserve a sense of perspective about their children's problems. Empathy should be balanced by good sense.

● While many of the 'boundaries' we adopt when bringing up children may not be for constructive reasons, some are and Pisceans should think carefully about what is best.

● Occasionally Pisces parents – especially Pisces fathers – need to be more reliable. Think of the hurt you are inflicting if you do not stand by your promises and responsibilities.

● Pisces children should never be badgered to be more rational or predictable. Their perceptions of life need to be honoured, although if they differ considerably from what is generally accepted, a balance should be sought.

● Parents of Pisceans should not pressurise these children, however subtly, to conform to their own expectations.

● Be honest with feelings, especially when there is a young Piscean in the house. They will know when something isn't right.

4 Friendships and the single life

The reality is that every human being is broken and vulnerable. How strange that we should ordinarily feel compelled to hide our wounds when we are all wounded!

M. Scott Peck, *The Different Drum*

Friendships are important to all of us. However, those who are single often find they have more time on their hands to devote to friends. Pisceans who have families can find themselves rather drained by the wishes of all and sundry. However, Pisceans do need a wide circle of friends to stimulate them and offer them the picture of 'life's rich tapestry' that they need.

■ PISCES AS A FRIEND

Pisceans usually know how their friends are feeling and will do their best to enter into friend's states of mind, sometimes to console, at others to celebrate triumphs. They may find that when they phone, Pisces says 'I thought it was you'. This sign usually has at least a trace of the psychic, and if this doesn't stretch to spotting the ghost of Great Uncle Frederick on the stairs it will almost certainly encompass an uncanny knack of knowing whether friends are going to call, or what sort of day they have had. You Pisceans can see it, or sense it, in their aura. You may bring out the tarot cards or cast the runes if friends want to know their 'fortune'. You have a great need to ensure that others are comfortable and happy. You will listen endlessly, with an attentive expression, to their tales of woe. Deep inside you may be bored, and your mind may be wandering, but they'd never guess!

You will often silently implore friends' help by looking forlorn, but there is a fear of taking advantage in your sign. If you are troubled, you will only feel worse if you feel you are 'too much' for your friends, and you may need to have your worries and fears coaxed out of you. Friends should refrain from giving advice – many people feel they can 'sort out' the problems of Pisces by straight talking and common sense, when what Pisces needs is empathy and support. You may seem accommodating, but you do hate to be invaded and will certainly retreat, even becoming unavailable for weeks to someone who has upset you. You rarely encourage confrontation but can become sharp if pushed to far, and then friends may find that things they didn't know about themselves or thought were their best-kept secret have been an open book to you all along, and they are the ones hearing the 'home truths'.

All Pisceans need to withdraw at times, because you take on too much and become desperate for peace and quiet or time to drift and dream. Many Pisces people take their phones off the hook for certain periods, although at others they seem the most gregarious of people. There are usually two sides to Mer-people in this respect. Pisceans need to submerge to incommunicable depths and if you are disturbed at these times you may be erratic, unwelcoming, even rude, and evasive. You may tell lies to get yourself some space, but when you are ready to 'come back' you may apologise for your behaviour.

Sensitive and tactful, you are nonetheless generally honest about your feelings. However, you will go to great lengths not to cause hurt and to 'sugar the pill'. If you are forced to tell friends that their new romance lacks promise, or their new outfit lacks taste, you will do your utmost simultaneously to life their spirits and offer help in finding something better. You are often really good at this, and can arrange the lives of others much better than your own. However, you do love your friends to be protective and caring towards you – how you behave towards others is an indication of how you would like to be treated.

Pisceans sometimes shut themselves away for long periods feeling 'misunderstood' and then wonder why they are lonely. Mostly you are friendly to just about everyone – except for the occasional character to whom you may take an unaccountable dislike. Later on, it usually transpires that this person wasn't to be trusted. General advice to Pisces could be that you need to learn to be a friend to yourself and to trust that people will not be put off by your 'selfishness' but will feel even more at ease with you. Pisceans can be entertaining, witty, and funny and you come into your own when you feel accepted.

■ PISCES AND THE SINGLE LIFE

Generally Pisces doesn't like to live alone; you may like to *be* alone for long periods, but having no one in your life can be a desert, and you may go around with an air of melancholy 'alone and palely loitering'. However, it is deeply necessary for you to be alone in life, at least for a short while, in order that you may orientate yourself and find your own special star to sail by. You can manage alone quite well, and once a faith in life and your own capabilities is achieved, you can be really excited at the sheer scope, variety and opportunity in life. There is magic everywhere once this is perceived, and you are then in a much better position to form a relationship where there is no hidden agenda of neediness, dependency, identity support or merging.

Pisces will always need a purpose in life, and this can sometimes be best discovered when Mer-people are single and not accommodating excessively to the demands of partner and family. Companions need to be chosen with care, for you can be readily influenced by the psychic field of others. This does not mean that you are easily led astray, but more that you can find your moods affected by others. You must have the courage of your convictions, and if someone doesn't make you feel 'good', stay away.

If you are single, you must make the best of your time, for you are adaptable and likely to form a partnership of some sort sooner rather than later. In particular, time alone can be most valuable to find your 'vocation': not necessarily a job but something meaning-ful or 'spiritual' which all Pisceans need in their lives. This means you must find a way to connect with something that is greater than yourself and gives you a place in the cosmos – this could be a reli-gion, either orthodox or unorthodox, an art or creative purpose or something more nebulous that means 'finding yourself' at some level. Once you have found this you possess an inviolable strength and something that is an eternal companion and source of support and sustenance.

You can be a person of extremes or one of the crowd. Sometimes you are artistic and noticeably 'arty', or sometimes conventional. Often the 'alternative' scene may appeal and you can be avid in the pursuit of enlightenment, unusual experience or expansion of consciousness. In this you can be inspired or deluded and you must take that precious time alone to reflect upon this. Mer-people must not give too much away in terms of time or attention, in the wrong quarters, for time is important and precious. In short, a single Pisces has the opportunity to find him or herself, with all that may mean; someone who has found that is never alone again.

■ PRACTICE AND CHANGE ■

● Try to rid yourself of the fear that you may be 'too much' for your friends. A friend who isn't prepared to help may be one you can do without.

● If you feel misunderstood or miserable, it is a mistake to shut yourself off. The world won't come knocking at your door. You must be direct about your needs and proactive about securing friends.

● Practise ways of saying 'no'. You *must not* agree to do too many things, please too many people, or you will be lost to yourself.

● Be your own best friend. You will have more to give this way, and anyway, don't you deserve it?

● Try not to fear being alone, for it is where you will find your greatest truth. Saying this will not take away the hollow feeling, but have faith.

● Always choose your companions with care. Friends are important and influential. Give anyone who does not make you feel good, encouraged and positive a wide berth. Helping people is nourishing to you – being drained, exploited, demeaned, denied, criticised, undermined or badgered is not.

5 Career

I like work; it fascinates me. I can sit and look at it for hours.

J. K. Jerome

Laborare est orare – To work is to pray

Latin proverb

Piscean ambiguity is in evidence in the sphere of work: when it comes to the boring and the onerous, Pisces' favourite word is *'Manana'*; when the Piscean imagination is appealed to, Pisces will often acquire the strength of ten and the languid, laid-back persona gives way to a darting silverfish that may seem to be in several places at once. It all depends upon motivation.

Mer-people tend to be better than most at performing repetitive tasks because you are able to 'switch off' and let your imagination wander. However, what Pisces really needs is a vocation – a sense that what you are doing is deeply meaningful.

■ TRADITIONAL PISCES CAREERS

The common denominator with most of the careers suitable for Pisceans is that they have a fluidity (literal or metaphoric) and a creative, artistic or healing quality. Pisces careers include:

- priest/ess
- healing professions
- medium
- social worker
- charity work
- fortune teller

- fisher
- artist
- chiropodist
- poet
- counsellor
- dancer
- hypnotist
- the navy
- writer
- shoemaker or seller
- actor
- work with animals and in institutions
- photographer

■ WHAT TO LOOK FOR IN YOUR WORK

Most people work in large financial institutions, sales offices, shops and factories. Relatively few of us can choose a profession, train for it and find a fulfilling lifestyle, and as time progresses this is becoming more elusive.

To help you find a job that suits you, you need to bear in mind the spirit of what is recommended, not the specific occupation. One office job is not like another, one shop selling fashions may differ enormously from one down the street in terms of environment and opportunity. If you are a Pisces you need to make sure of several things when seeking employment:

- You like the people you work with: they are nice to you, supportive, friendly and open, and the atmosphere is pleasant.
- You are not subject to relentless pressure (other than self-imposed). You may work well with bursts of pressure interspersed with periods of calm but a perpetually frantic atmosphere will deplete you.
- There is no one breathing down your neck, criticising, demanding and whip-cracking.
- Schedules are fluid; flexi-time would suit you or some job where emphasis is on results, not timekeeping and 'putting in the hours'.

- You will enjoy variety in your work, perhaps travel, meeting people, etc.
- While you can adapt to a job that is basically 'pleasant' you will only ever be really happy in your work if it is a vocation and calls forth something that is within you.

So there is no need to feel that you have to look for a specifically Piscean job. Many Pisces can't dance to save their lives and would get seasick at the mere thought of a 'life on the ocean wave'. Look for something that suits in its content and atmosphere, rather than its label. If you don't like where you are, don't blame yourself – make a change for the better.

■ CINDERELLA

It is true that Cinders is principally a female figure, but there are plenty of male varieties, whom we might call 'little boy lost'. This type of Piscean swims in the waters of company and office like a mournful minnow in a large tank. These people may be doing their job valiantly or, more likely, giving that impression, but they are crying out for rescue. One day the Fairy Godmother will wave her wand and all this boring stuff will disappear and along will come the handsome prince – or rather the recording contract/modelling job/ commission to sculpt a statue – and Cinders will swan off to the life of glamour that is his or her true birthright.

Waiting to be 'discovered' is a classic Piscean trap. Dusty offices and backstreet shops are full of ageing Cinderellas still waiting, hoping, growing grey and, if the truth were known, embittered as the gap between what they dream about and what is possible widens to a chasm. To some people, especially in youth, these are romantic figures who often inspire others with a faith in life. Equally they may earn contempt and pity. These people may console themselves with the thought 'I'm just a dreamer', but it's cold comfort when the alarm rings on another grey morning. So, if this is you, you are just being too passive. What are you going to *do*? You must go out and find that glass slipper for your own slender foot.

■ THE ANDROID

We have mentioned the 'vacant' Pisces in earlier chapters – he or she who has wiped out all the 'Intimations of Immortality' and consented to be reprogrammed according to 'average expectations'. Here we have Cinderella's opposite: a Pisces who has traded hopes and dreams for acceptable mediocrity and sold his or her soul to the company or cultural norms. All that remains may be a vacuous grin, like the Cheshire Cat, that lingers after all other personality traits have vanished. This sort of Pisces is best avoided, unless colleagues are prepared to lay some depth charges, because there can be an air of suffocation and subtle negativity underneath the genial manner that is quite discouraging.

Pisceans who have shaped themselves to an acceptable model and lost their essence are common. The majority of Pisceans do this in some way, at some point, and the trick is to catch yourself doing it and stop. Develop an awareness, an investigative curiosity, about where and how your strings are being pulled and keep away from influences that you decide are harmful. Meditate and reflect upon what you truly are, truly want. *Why* exactly are you doing this job and where is it written that this is how you should be? Are you fulfilled? Do you *want* to do this for another month, another year? Don't tell yourself nothing better is possible – that's just negative reprogramming. Wipe the slates clean and invite the real you in.

■ THE PISCES BOSS

The Pisces boss is rarely a natural authority figure, although some will maintain an aloof posture rather than give this away. Pisceans often actively avoid positions of responsibility, but some have 'greatness thrust upon them' perhaps because they are plain brilliant at something. Typically, this is an approachable, genial boss, understanding and humorous. Usually it is quite possible to appeal to this person's sympathies, and time off may be generously given to visit sick relatives or take the dog to the vet. Be careful, however. Employees shouldn't imagine they can take advantage, because Pisces will probably know if they are lying. Pisces understands a little lack of directness and values employees who are imaginative and creative, but when the chips are down, this is a survivor. In times of stress, it's the reliable, practical people who are the 'bread and butter', and Pisces can usually supply all the originality one office requires. A smile and a joke are no guarantees of security. Tactfully, with many sincere expressions of regret, compliments and promises of good references, Pisces will let troublesome employees go.

The Pisces boss can be creative and dramatic, and much more concerned with art (or healing) than profit. However, she or he can sense market trends and often has a nose for a good deal. Pisces is shrewd and good at investigation. Fortified by success, some Piscean bosses are noncomformist, while others maintain a rather insipid image. However, this is a person of surprises. Words often come best to Pisces when angry, and some Pisceans know instinctively that they must use their anger to maximum advantage because at other times their tender heart will get in the way. Pisces enraged is a person capable of sarcasm, cutting diatribe and ruthless action. Employees should treat Piscean tolerance with respect.

However switched on the Pisces boss seems, the mystic isn't usually that far away. At heart this boss is a gentle person who wants most of all to believe that the world is a benign place and the age of enchantment is still with us. If employees show that they are practical and reliable and that they can do all the things that Pisces secretly fears they can't manage – and show also that there is a corner in them that fantasises and wishes upon a star – then Pisces will see that they, too, have a foot in both worlds, and they may just have a job for life.

■ THE PISCES EMPLOYEE

Often sensitive and unsure of themselves even when they are talented, Pisces employees can be injured by a thoughtless word to the point where they do not function at anything like their level of capability. Sometimes these people will be miserable misfits and some Pisceans can appear servile, but they will deeply resent being ordered about and they may pretend to work for several months before swimming off somewhere where they are more appreciated.

Pisceans can be methodical, reliable and loyal, and if they are well-treated they will jump through hoops and pull rabbits out of hats. Pisces likes to be needed and appreciated. This person probably has considerable skill in some sphere that may be additional to what employers know about and what they hired Pisces for. Pisces is easily bored and sometimes endlessly creative and resourceful, so employers should respect this fact, and make use of it. Pisces is often good at sorting out trouble in the workplace, by dint of giving everyone a fair and understanding hearing.

Pisceans need a pleasant working environment and a calm atmosphere to function at their best. Physical surroundings need to be attractive – give Pisceans nothing to look at but a bank of grey filing cabinets and they will become withdrawn and dismal.

The emotional atmosphere should be as harmonious as possible, too. Pisceans should be given as much freedom as possible. Often Pisceans like to know exactly what is expected of them but not how and when to do it. Pisces will usually understand boss and colleagues quite well, while Pisces may be an eternal mystery. Employers shouldn't dismiss what they can't quite comprehend. One day Pisces may come up with a dazzling idea that will catapult everyone into the Big League.

■ WHEN UNEMPLOYMENT STRIKES

Many Pisceans have a 'feeling' that they are going to lose their job, and if they are wise they make provision. However, Pisceans can be worriers and it may be hard to distinguish between intuition and mere anxiety. When they really are without a job, Pisceans may catch the express to dreamland and stay there, fantasising about lottery wins, unexpected legacies and other forms of rescue.

This sort of situation can bring out the best in Pisces, or the worst. The 'best' means that Pisces, worldly-wise and accepting, shrugs his or her shoulders philosophically and makes the best of a bad job. In the interim, Pisces will get down to writing the book, finishing the painting or redecorating the hallway. This is a chance for a real overhaul, and so Pisces may opt for a change of direction, rather grateful that Fate has made the difficult decision. The 'worst' on the other hand, means escapism, staying up late at night, getting up later and later in the morning and generally becoming dissociated from 'normal' life to the point where it may be increasingly difficult to get back on track. Pisces may wallow in self-pity and become despairing and even self-destructive. If you are an unemployed Pisces use this as a chance to make changes. Jot down your dreams and schemes, talk to people, play with ideas but keep things in proportion. This has happened for a reason – give the reason time to make itself apparent.

■ SELF-EMPLOYMENT AND OTHER MATTERS

Not all work relies on a company and an employer for there are
many other approaches. Pisceans are often excellent at working
freelance, for they far prefer to set their own pace and rhythm,
which may vary from day to day, and often fulfil commitments
much better when not tied to routine. However, Pisceans can lack
direction and may fail to use their time profitably. If you are a
Pisces with a specific talent, it is usually better to have an agent,
either formal or informal, to act for you. You are rarely good at self-
promotion, although you can be excellent at promoting someone
else in whom you believe. Pisceans work much better if they have a
commission that shows someone else has faith in them and wants
their work, and from that point they can be self-motivating. The
right partner may be a great help to you – someone who appreciates
and encourages and someone whom you can support in turn.

■ PRACTICE AND CHANGE ■

- Give a thought to what your 'vocation' is. Keep the question
  – and your eyes – open.

- Money is rarely your priority, but you *must* force yourself to
  sell yourself well, and to ensure that you are paid fairly.

- In your work you need a congenial atmosphere, freedom
  and scope for your talents, rather than a high salary.

- Do not waste time hoping for 'rescue' while the floodwaters
  rise. Use your ingenuity and paddle your canoe.

- You like to feel part of a larger 'whole' but being a cog in a
  faceless company will hardly satisfy your urge for meaning.
  Are you confusing security with fulfilment?

- If you are unemployed, or self-employed, you will need an
  'anchor'.

6 Healthy, wealthy – and wise?

We cannot heal without willing to be hurt

M. Scott Peck, *The Different Drum*

■ HEALTH

Astrological observations on health are quite difficult, because health is a complex and sensitive area, influenced by many factors. What may we usefully say about the health of Pisceans in general?

Pisceans have a reputation of giving too freely of themselves, of not erecting sufficiently substantial barriers against the encroachment of other people's demands and feelings and of being, in general, too sensitive. It is indeed the case that Pisceans often seem to take the weight of the world upon their shoulders and they can certainly become depressed and tired because of this. It is well known that if one becomes too dispirited the immune system suffers and one is more open to illness. Pisces may suffer from colds, pains in the limbs and a feeling of exhaustion. It is not an exaggeration to state that the negativity of other people can make Pisces ill. However, the urge to heal is strong in Pisces, and the act of healing, to a certain extent, can have a healing effect upon the healer. Pisces often has a great deal to give. The trick is to strike a balance, and not to give beyond a reasonable amount. Limits must be set and not breached.

Because Piscean perceptions are so wide ranging, the stress can be depressing in itself. Pisceans who become discouraged and depressed need to hold on to the belief that however black things may look, this isn't a useful – or in some respects even real – perspective. Often the act of soldiering on 'as if' does make things better. Usually the cloud passes.

Healthy forms of support are essential for Pisces. Many people assume that strength and self-preservation are matters of standing alone – not so. To be able to find the right help is adult and sensible, and not the same as dependency. Pisces may seek this in friendships, or sometimes in therapy. Mer-people also need to beware that their forms of 'escape' are not injurious. It can be all too easy to turn to alcohol or drugs because they anaesthetise pain – unfortunately they send all the aware and alive bits to sleep as well. The only way to avoid this is not to start, and if you've started, stop. Use your imagination to retain in your mind the image of what this could do to your life.

Pisceans can – or should – have an instinct for sound nutrition. Often they are good at sorting out the diets of other people but neglect their own. Plan what you are going to eat, and if this means scraping a couple of carrots and chopping fruit just after breakfast, that is far better than waiting until you are worn out and reaching for a chocolate bar for lunch. Pisceans often have a problem knowing when to stop – here the hedonistic aspect of the sign takes over! A little of what you fancy does you good, but if you regularly overeat or drink, you need to ask yourself what you are lacking in life that you need this as a compensation?

Feet and fundamentals

Pisces is said to rule the feet; uncomfortable or injured feet are debilitating. Pisceans tend to have 'noticeable' feet – either graceful as a dancer's or spread out like tree-roots! They also love nice shoes – as many as possible, and often chosen for their attractiveness and glamour rather than for comfort. Louise Hay in *You Can Heal Your Life* states that the feet 'represent our understanding – of ourselves, of life, of others', and these are Piscean matters. Foot problems can show fear of life's next step, ingrown toenails may indicate worry about one's right to move forward. So something as simple as sensible care for the feet can mean we feel generally more confident, decisive and grounded. The soles of the feet have reflex associations with the rest of the body; Pisceans may enjoy reflexology.

■ MONEY

Not known as a sign that is 'good' with money, Pisces may give it away, lend it or invest it unwisely, or simply not know how to attract it. You are often not sure of, or guilty about, your earning power, and tend to 'sell yourself short'. Many Mer-people feel that money should not be a prime factor, because it is unspiritual, and so they may condition themselves to poverty – and then feel sorry for themselves! Pisceans like money just as much as the next person, for you love comfort and beauty. Amassing money for its own sake, however, is rarely a Piscean pleasure – unless there is a lot of fear and neurosis in the personality. You need to remind yourself that money is simply energy, or power, solidified, and if you want to do certain things in life you need it. There is no need to feel guilty.

An effective ploy is always to take advice on money matters, or simply to hand them over to a trusted helper. One Pisces writer always consults her Capricorn husband regarding anything to do with money and then forces herself to carry out his recommendations. This has meant that she has been paid for all sorts of things that she would otherwise have done free. Intrestingly, Pisceans may be very good indeed as agents, getting excellent rates for other people!

Pisceans, as we know, are not good at keeping within limits. Because of this you may run up debts through over-spending on the glamorous, or be over-generous and give too much away. You should protect yourself from too many charity demands, for few Pisceans can resist the forlorn little dog or the tiny child with the frightened eyes, and will send off more than they can afford, to the detriment of the rest of the family. Again, you need to realise that you cannot set the world to rights. In addition, you must remind yourself that what you, and others, fondly call 'generosity' may have more to do with some form of guilt, and you need to look at that sternly, for it is destructive.

Pisceans often find it is best to 'trick' themselves about their money, simply telling themselves they earn less than they do, putting money in inaccessible accounts and avoiding credit cards like the plague – to Pisces these are 'flexible fiends' that give Mer-people enough elastic to hang themselves!

■ WISDOM

Pisces is synonymous with wisdom, carrying the wealth and sorrow of all human experience inside. Pisceans often seem confused, gullible or foolish, and this can be because not all of you are prepared to respond to the potentials of your sign. However, it may be because to you certain things don't matter; you may know perfectly well when you are being 'taken in' and not really mind. It is usually hard to fool, or even to surprise, you. Pisceans are almost unshockable. Usually you are deeply forgiving, because you can understand almost anything (however, in the once-in-a-lifetime event of Pisces judging against someone, the shutters are capable of going down forever and the offender classified as inhuman). To a Pisces who is truly 'in tune', the fact that this world is temporary and even illusory is a real perception – all things must pass. However, Pisceans should not use this as a reason for not engaging in life, for we are here for a purpose.

■ PRACTICE AND CHANGE ■

Health

● Keep your exposure to negative people within limits. Seek out people who make you laugh, who are positive and with whom you can enjoy life.

● If you feel discouraged, tell yourself this is not a real perception of life, but a temporary angst. Do not allow discouragement to compound discouragement. Pamper yourself so you are ready to go forward when you feel better.

● Healthy support is essential. Make no bones about seeking this; it is an intelligent step, and should be done consciously.

● You may need to get organised if you are to look after your own creature comforts – for example, plan and prepare food in advance.

● Look after your feet! Properly shod feet mean someone who intends to get somewhere.

Wealth

● Try to dismantle any guilt or reticence you have over money. The use of money determines its value; you can't do anything without it, and you are entitled to be comfortable.

● If you wish to give to charity, set aside a sensible regular sum. Do not excede this, and review it from time to time.

● Take advice about money. Someone else may be far better at looking after your interests than you are. You might try a reciprocal arrangement, where you act as agent for another, and vice-versa, for you may be more fervent about someone else's rights than your own.

7

Style and leisure

Pleasure is a freedom-song,
But it is not freedom.
It is the blossoming of your desires
But it is not their fruit . . .
It is the caged taking wing,
But it is not space encompassed . . .

Kahlil Gibran, *The Prophet*

■ YOUR LEISURE

Pisceans need 'play' essentially to take them out of themselves and into a wider universe where the commonplace can, in some sense, be left behind. Mer-people love to 'lose' themselves in a good book or film, but often something active can be more beneficial. Even benign forms of 'escape' means one has to come back to the daily grind with a bump. Essentially it is better to be involved in something creative, because then, when one 'returns' one brings something with one in the way of genuine regeneration, relaxation, enlargement of the spirit and inspiration. Pastimes should leave one with more energy, not less, and a feeling of healthy fatigue.

Pisces can be an artistic sign, and practically all Pisceans love and appreciate the beautiful, even if you do not actively create it. You may need to free yourself of expectations and conventions before your natural talent can flow. Activities to consider particularly are music and dance of all types, drama, painting and perhaps making glass, or staining glass, and photography. Many Pisceans have some form of psychic power and are often interested in subjects that are occult for you love mysteries and your inner natures resonate to the unexplained. All forms of fortune telling or even mediumship may attract, and lots of Pisceans have talents in this respect. Always ensure you are fully grounded after your activities, and take the appropriate steps to protect yourself, whatever line you pursue. You should be careful you do not open yourself too much to stray energies and maintain a balanced lifestyle. However, some Pisceans are extremely sceptical and disinterested or scornful about these subjects. This may be in order to protect themselves – these Pisceans may feel they have to justify their interests and beliefs. It may be better if they can free themselves from such constraints.

This is rarely a competitive sign, but Pisceans can enjoy sports and while you might not be particularly hung up on winning, you like to do well and may be afraid of making a fool of yourself. You enjoy the sensation of fluid and expert movement – again, dancing is especially featured. All water sports are traditionally recommended. Swimming is excellent exercise, and one which Pisces may naturally enjoy.

Holidays

Piscean tastes in holidays are extremely varied. Generally, Pisces likes the chance to relax – a glass of wine on a balmy evening beside the pool, with some good friends and music can be heaven to Pisces. However, Pisceans can become restless and bored. Any holiday should include some exploration and adventure. You need to get away from the banal and everyday – some Pisceans love the idea of being miles from the beaten track in remote rusticity, but lack of comfort is rarely popular. The transfer of family chores and bickerings to a more exotic location will do absolutely nothing for you, and canned entertainment on a holiday camp wins few prizes.

When abroad there should be an experience of local flavour – you love to rub shoulders with the locals and try to get into the feeling of what it is *really* like to live and work in this part of the world. Pisces women especially should be freed from catering and enabled to play glamour-puss. Holidays do not have to be taken abroad. What is essential for you is that you feel 'taken out of yourself' and that the holiday has been some form of experience. Romance is important, and a 'fantasy holiday' on a desert island, or similar, may appeal. Many Pisceans are deeply stirred by scenery and seascapes. Who Pisceans holiday with is as important as where.

▪ YOUR STYLE

As a Pisces your style is likely to be atmospheric and imaginative. Ambience, delicate lighting, tasteful and well-chosen décor with a hint of the mysterious or unusual are characteristic. Liking for privacy and rest may influence you to choose net curtains. There may be figures of dragons, dolphins and mermaids with decorative objects in glass, and candles of all shapes and sizes favoured. Scarves may be tastefully draped to soften corners, and there may be paintings by pre-Raphaelites or Impressionists on the walls. A taste for the 'ethnic' or 'alternative' may be in evidence, and there is likely to be a selection of books and magazines to hand. Pisceans often have a talent for making people feel comfortable. Many are animal lovers and there will be a cosy nook for the pet cat or dog. Despite your reputation, you are rarely chaotic, and while clinical tidiness is unlikely (although not unknown) you tend to like a certain amount of order – perhaps because you sense that total disorder may be only around the corner, and you need some structure to keep your mind in gear! A place for everything is important, although not everything will need to be in its place, all of the time.

Mer-people should make a point of tracking down anything in the environment that is discordant or unappealing and make no bones about getting rid of it. Do not hang on to Great Aunt Ethel's hideous vase 'for sentimental reasons' because it will get you down. Convenience and pragmatism should always be balanced by aesthetic appeal. What is on the floor may be of especial importance to Pisces, so invest in sumptuous, wall-to-wall carpets. A warm and luxurious bathroom, with a selection of oils and soft towels will be especially pleasant to Pisces. Many Pisceans like cooking, and will love the appearance of shelves full of spices and herbs in a window box. In the kitchen avoid the harsh and clinical. Put the food processor away in the cupboard, so there is room to feast your eyes on your selection of extra-virgin olive oils and fine wines! Pastel or muted shades may be favoured in the home.

Clothes should be comfortable, but also glamorous. Pisces people often love dressing up, and may enjoy looking one minute like a gypsy, next minute like a chef, next minute like a Hollywood starlet. Lounging-around outfits, relaxing yet seductive, are very much Pisces style. Men may like to wear robes, or thin and loose cotton trousers with colourful silk shirts. Lots of Pisceans like to go barefoot around the house. Flowing styles, lace and chiffon can also appeal. Because you like to play-act, you may enjoy wearing tailored suits and you can be 'sharp' dressers on occasion, but usually you are only too pleased to get home and 'slip into something more comfortable'. Pisceans have a reputation for collecting shoes, and may have a fine array of footwear in many colours and styles.

When you are choosing purchases for yourself or your home think subtle appeal, intriguing, mysterious, different, comfortable, soothing, evocative, beautiful, artistic, relaxing. Your tastes may be eclectic. Try to resist impulse buying, or you may end up with a hotch-potch. When making choices always give yourself time to relax and visualise how things will look. Is this a whim, or something that will appeal in the future and complement what you already have? It may be best for you to shop on your own, unless you are sure that the person with you has similar tastes. It may be too easy to 'tune in' to what someone else likes and find, later on, that you would really have preferred something else.

■ PRACTICE AND CHANGE ■

- When choosing pastimes, remember that something that actively involves you is likely to inspire and energise you.

- Developing your intuition and/or psychic skills may be appealing and life enhancing. However, always keep things in proportion.

- Remember that moderate sporting activity actually *gives* you energy. It can leave you feeling energetic and cheerful, even if it seemed like a gargantuan task at the start.

- Your holidays should involve a little romance, good company and a flavour of the unusual. Plan to be 'taken out of yourself'.

- Your surroundings should be subtle, atmospheric and contain plenty of beautiful things. Comfort, too, is paramount. Do not hesitate to get rid of the discordant.

- Shop alone, for then you will be better able to think straight. Guard against buying 'bits' for you could end up with a wardrobe of things that don't match. Take the time to plan outfits and colour schemes.

- Too much clutter will make it hard to decide what to wear. If you are keeping something for 'sentimental reasons', put it away and look at it from time to time. Don't feel guilty about getting rid of 'mistakes'; they are just a bind and a reminder of misjudgement.

Appendix 1

■ PISCES COMBINED WITH MOON SIGN

Our 'birth sign' or 'star sign' refers to the sign of the zodiac occupied by the Sun when we were born. This is also called our 'Sun sign' and this book is concerned with Pisces as a Sun sign. However, as we saw in the Introduction, a horoscope means much more than the position of the Sun alone. All the other planets have to be taken into consideration by an astrologer. Of great importance is the position of the Moon.

The Moon completes a tour of the zodiac in about twenty-eight days, changing sign every two days or so. The Moon relates to our instincts, responses, reactions, habits, comfort zone and 'where we live' emotionally – and sometimes physically. It is very important in respect of our intuitional abilities and our capacity to feel part of our environment, but because what the Moon rules is usually non-verbal and non-rational; it has been neglected. This has meant that our lives have become lop-sided. Learning to be friends with our instincts can lead to greater well-being and wholeness.

Consult the table on page 82 to find which sign the Moon was in, at the time of your birth. This, combined with your Sun sign is a valuable clue to deeper understanding.

Find your Moon number

Look up your month and day of birth. Then read across to find your
personal Moon number. Now go to Chart 2, below.

January		February		March		April		May		June	
1,2	1	1,2	3	1,2	3	1,2	5	1,2	6	1,2	8
3,4	2	3,4	4	3,4	4	3,4	6	3,4	7	3,4	9
5,6	3	5,6	5	5,6	5	5,6	7	5,6	8	5,6,7	10
7,8	4	7,8	6	7,8	6	7,8	8	7,8	9	8,9	11
9,10	5	9,10,11	7	9,10	7	9,10,11	9	9,10	10	10,11,12	12
11,12	6	12,13	8	11,12	8	12,13	10	11,12,13	11	13,14	1
13,14	7	14,15	9	13,14	9	14,15,16	11	14,15,16	12	15,16,17	2
15,16,17	8	16,17,18	10	15,16,17	10	17,18	12	17,18	1	18,19	3
18,19	9	19,20	11	18,19	11	19,20,21	1	19,20	2	20,21	4
20,21	10	21,22,23	12	20,21,22	12	22,23	2	21,22,23	3	22,23	5
22,23,24	11	24,25	1	23,24,25	1	24,25	3	24,25	4	24,25	6
25,26	12	26,27,28	2	26,27	2	26,27,28	4	26,27	5	26,27	7
27,28,29	1	29	3	28,29	3	29,30	5	28,29	6	28,29,30	8
30,31	2			30,31	4			30,31	7		

July		August		September		October		November		December	
1,2	9	1	10	1,2	12	1,2	1	1,2,3	3	1,2	4
3,4	10	2,3	11	3,4	1	3,4	2	4,5	4	3,4	5
5,6,7	11	4,5,6	12	5,6,7	2	5,6	3	6,7	5	5,6	6
8,9	12	7,8	1	8,9	3	7,8,9	4	8,9	6	7,8,9	7
10,11,12	1	9,10	2	10,11	4	10,11	5	10,11	7	10,11	8
13,14	2	11,12,13	3	12,13	5	12,13	6	12,13	8	12,13	9
15,16	3	14,15	4	14,15	6	14,15	7	14,15	9	14,15	10
17,18	4	16,17	5	16,17	7	16,17	8	16,17,18	10	16,17	11
19,20	5	18,19	6	18,19	8	18,19	9	19,20	11	18,19,20	12
21,22,23	6	20,21	7	20,21,22	9	20,21	10	21,22,23	12	21,22	1
24,25	7	22,23	8	23,24	10	22,23,24	11	24,25	1	23,24,25	2
26,27	8	24,25	9	25,26,27	11	25,26	12	26,27,28	2	26,27	3
28,29	9	26,27,28	10	28,29	12	27,28,29	1	29,30	3	28,29	4
30,31	10	29,30	11	30	1	30,31	2			30,31	5
		31	12								

Find your Moon sign

Find your year of birth. Then read across to the column of your Moon number.
Where they intersect shows your Moon sign.

Birth year				Moon number										
				1	2	3	4	5	6	7	8	9	10	11
1900	1919	1938	1957	1976	Leo	Vir	Lib	Sco	Sag	Cap	Aqu	Pis	Ari	Tau	Gem
1901	1920	1939	1958	1977											
1902	1921	1940	1959	1978											
1903	1922	1941	1960	1979											
1904	1923	1942	1961	1980											
1905	1924	1943	1962	1981											
1906	1925	1944	1963	1982											
1907	1926	1945	1964	1983											
1908	1927	1946	1965	1984											
1909	1928	1947	1966	1985											
1910	1929	1948	1967	1986											
1911	1930	1949	1968	1987											
1912	1931	1950	1969	1988											
1913	1932	1951	1970	1989											
1914	1933	1952	1971	1990											
1915	1934	1953	1972	1991											
1916	1935	1954	1973	1992											
1917	1936	1955	1974	1993											
1918	1937	1956	1975	1994											

Ari	Tau	Gem	Can	Leo	Vir	Lib	Sco	Sag	Cap	Aqu	Pis

Pisces Sun / Pisces Moon

Dreamy and impressionable, it is important for you to have space in your life to escape into a world of your own. You are a deeply sympathetic person, and usually strongly aware of your own feelings – indeed you may become immersed in them. You may choose to escape into a world of fantasy, and need to be careful to use this positively and creatively, for there may be a temptation to intensify the experience through alcohol or drugs. It is most important to learn to give to yourself in a healthy way, not to try to elicit sympathy always from others, or lose yourself in their needs. It is possible for you to be dynamic and artistic; you have a great need to take the universe in your embrace. Seek your spiritual source and make your dreams count.

Pisces Sun / Aries Moon

Spontaneous and enthusiastic, there is something of the innocent child within you, and also an ingredient of the eternally wise and ancient. Sometimes these two sit well together. At others you may be appalled at where your impulsiveness has got you now! You like to initiate things, but you also need to see the deeper meanings in what you do, and if they are not present you lose interest. You can be selfish and irrational or generous and actively helpful. It is important to you to understand your real needs, for you may alternate between being demanding or giving everything away. Ensure that the stimulation you seek is of a healthy kind and that you are not giving double messages: 'I can do without anyone' alternating with 'I am desperately lost and needy'. Some form of creative endeavour is essential to your well-being as it will act as the anchor you need and give you a sense of reality.

Pisces Sun / Taurus Moon

Although you may give the impression of being laid back, you are capable of achieving a great deal, when you so choose. Human warmth, closeness and security are important to you and you are capable of backing up your understanding with constructive action. You may be rather on the self-indulgent side and you perhaps need a fair bit of input from other people in order to make you feel worthwhile. Your self-esteem is not high and you may alternate between self-pity and over self-sufficiency. Those who do not know you well may see you as a caring 'coper' but inside your appetite for approval, love and support is as insatiable as a puppy's! You are probably artistic in some form, a good host/ess, gardener or cook. You may be afraid to let go and move on in difficult situations. However, you are both extremely capable practically, while having the capacity for deep spiritual and emotional strength and awareness. Have faith!

Pisces Sun / Gemini Moon

You are possibly quite an elusive character: sometimes you want to get close, at other times you want freedom. You are probably restless, talkative and responsive. You are good at lending a sympathetic ear, and may have a talent for cheering people up. However, you can be changeable and contrary, rationalising your own feelings so they have little hope of being satisfied, scattering yourself too widely, sampling from many pots and driving yourself and others crazy by your unpredictability. It is yourself you are at odds with, not the world. Give yourself a chance to reconnect with your deepest feelings by stilling the chatter, once in a while. You are probably good with words; take the time to choose words that are going to express what you want and need, and make sure that all those stimulating activities nourish you at all levels, not just mentally.

Pisces Sun / Cancer Moon

Kind, sympathetic, charitable and understanding, there is sometimes a danger that you may lose all sense of your own needs in
catering to those of others. Conversely, you may expect other people to take care of you, prone to take the line of least resistance into
self-indulgence, or even self-pity. You like to live life to the full and
can be dynamic about exploiting your talents, because you are intuitive and able to see smooth ways of achieving your ends. You need
to make sure that the gratification you seek is healthy and strengthening; beware of substitutes such as over-eating or alcohol.
Relationships that are mutually nurturing are important to you and
you can best achieve these by being up front about what you need ,
rather than resorting to manipulation. Be prepared to love without
possessing, and especially make sure that you show love to yourself.

Pisces Sun / Leo Moon

You have the talent for drama, in more ways than one! You like to be
the centre of attention and you know instinctively how to achieve this.
Probably you are a colourful personality – poetic, artistic or buzzing
with ideas (that you do not always carry through to completion). You
can be warm, giving and spontaneous, or demanding and irrational. It
is important to you to be 'special' but you need to be careful that you
do not relinquish the limelight at the crucial point and end up frustrated. The impulse to self-sacrifice might sit awkwardly with the need
to dominate, causing you some internal stress. This may mean that
you 'dominate' through negative attention seeking. Remember, you
will never feel really lovable, however much applause you attract,
unless you love yourself. Give yourself permission to be spontaneous
and to be playful. Enjoy giving out your warmth, and enjoy also taking,
openly, the joy and triumph that comes your way.

Pisces Sun / Virgo Moon

You like everything in your life to be orderly and predictable and you expect high standards of yourself, and possibly others. You may drive yourself crazy trying to make sense of what cannot be tidied up and rendered rational, such as your feelings, intuitions and instinctive values. Thus you can be a real 'worrier' and may even develop neurotic habits as a substitute for being able to control what can never be controlled: life, change, the cosmos. On the other hand, you have the propensity to build a sensible and effectual framework in your life for what is inspirational, or even spiritual; you can also be highly effective and creative. It is all a question of getting the balance right. Give yourself permission to fail – we all do this. Be thorough about looking after your wants and needs as well as duties. Take note of your dreams for they could be revealing.

Pisces Sun / Libra Moon

Charming, conciliatory and a born peacemaker, you probably avoid trouble and confrontation like the plague. You are a lover of all that is beautiful and uplifting, and you will reason yourself out of your own feelings rather than cause strife. The trouble here is that feelings do not go away, they just go into hiding, and this can be stressful for you. Why should your needs be ignored? Good relationships are vital to your sense of well-being, but these can never come about if you put yourself last. Because you are understanding and empathic, you can find ways to assert yourself that will not upset others, if they are half reasonable. You are gifted with intuition and aesthetic sensitivity as well as the ability to be detached. Be kind to yourself also, and look for that true balance that comes from braving necessary disharmony at times.

Pisces Sun / Scorpio Moon

Passionate, deep-seeing and intense, you know how to get what you want and may find it easy to manipulate other people into giving it to you. Your sex drive may be strong and you are anything but superficial – indeed, your depths are fathomless and incommunicable and you greatly value your privacy. You know your own feelings well and this enables you to conceal them, when you wish, while understanding how other people are feeling; although you are sympathetic and kind it is not easy to pull the wool over your eyes and you prefer to help those who also help themselves. You have tremendous inner resources of determination and recuperation, and you should be able to find a way to draw upon them. Do not be afraid to go straight for what you want, because it is far simpler than manoeuvring others. If you wish to experience the most profound fulfilment, you may need to let go of that inner control once in a while.

Pisces Sun / Sagittarius Moon

Philosophical and optimistic, you like nothing better than to feel you have cheered someone up! You are kind and charitable, with a strong 'do-gooding' streak. Although you are emotional, you may prefer to believe that you do not feel certain things, for these may offend your ideals, and thus you may be frustrated and confused, your pride hurt by the fact that you have been taken advantage of. It is important to you to expand and explore, conceptually, emotionally and possibly physically, and you often try to do too much – thus, you may end up dissatisfied with having done nothing properly. It is vital that you develop your own moral code and a sense of what the 'divine' means to you. You may feel you are 'above' being needy, but unless you learn to give to yourself your suppressed feelings may sabotage your plans and leave you feeling you have let yourself down. This would be a great shame, for you are dynamic and imaginative.

Pisces Sun / Capricorn Moon

You are caring and efficient, and you are able to back up your imagination and compassion with some cold facts and sensible planning. You tend rather to be quiet and thoughtful. You often build solid foundations to your castles in the air – so why are you so self-critical and self-deprecating? Probably you are modest and turn away from the recognition of your accomplishments that you truly crave. You are protective of others but you do not sufficiently recognise your own vulnerability, and while you may feel upset, you shrug it off and get on with the job. Where is it written that you have to sacrifice yourself and put your own needs last? If you admit to and fully embrace your feelings you will discover a strength you did not know you had, and will be able to put more conviction and compassion into your endeavours.

Pisces Sun / Aquarius Moon

Yours is an abstract and even futuristic turn of mind, and your ideals are likely to be high. You have great compassion for humanity and may be something of a reformer. However, it is also possible that, while accepting the way everyone else feels, you may distance yourself from your own emotions and this can make your reactions erratic and unpredictable. You are an individualist, and you may find it at times almost impossible to express how you are feeling and what you are thinking. It is important for you to feel that you are unique, and also to belong to something greater than yourself. A wide circle of friends may appeal, but ensure that these support your true needs, not enable you to avoid them. Cultivate the inner freedom that embraces all feelings, and trust your intuition.

Appendix 2

■ ZODIACAL COMPATIBILITY

To assess fully the compatibility of two people the astrologer needs to have the entire chart of each individual, and while Sun-sign factors will be noticeable, there is a legion of other important points to be bourne in mind. Venus and Mercury are always close to the Sun, and while these are often in the Sun sign itself, so intensifying its effect, they may also fall in one of the signs lying on either side. So, as a Pisces you may have Venus and/or Mercury in Aquarius or Aries, and this will increase your empathy with these signs. In addition the Moon and all the other planets including the Ascendant and Midheaven need to be taken into account. So if you have always been drawn to Librans, maybe you have Moon or Ascendant in Libra.

In order to give a vivid character sketch things have to be stated graphically. You should look for the dynamics at work rather than be too literal about interpretation – for instance, you may find that Virgos complement your approach rather than rubbing you up the wrong way, but you may still be aware that there are considerable differences between you. It is up to the two of you whether a relationship works, for it can if you are both committed. There are always points of compatibility, and we are here to learn from each other.

On a scale of 1 (worst) to 4 (best), here is a table to assess instantly
the superficial compatibility rating between Pisces and companions:

Pisces 2	Virgo 1
Aries 3	Libra 1
Taurus 3	Scorpio 4
Gemini 2	Sagittarius 1
Cancer 4	Capricorn 4
Leo 3	Aquarius 2

■ PISCES COMPATIBILITIES

Pisces with Pisces

The two of you could wander around in a rosy haze and wake up to
find you're in a hopeless muddle. That won't matter at all as long as
you both have a laugh and work together at restoring order.
However, the danger is that you could blame each other. The one
who is outmanoeuvred may adopt a martyr stance – you can imagine
the rest.

As lovers   This can be utterly idyllic, as you both have the ability to
lose yourselves completely in the feeling and the act of love. Ms Pisces
is rapturous in the knowledge that at last she has met a truly emotional man, while Mr Pisces feels understood and supported. Pisces
partners are highly responsive. Because of this you could make each
other feel insecure. For your partnership to work you need to strive
for a sense of separateness. Understanding isn't likely to be a problem. Pragmatism and decision-making may be. Everything depends
on how you handle things when the web of fantasy breaks.

As friends   Pisces friendships work well, as there is less likelihood
of anyone feeling let down. Lots of empathy, emotional support
and shared interests.

As business partners   This isn't a good idea, unless one of you has plenty of planets in Earth or Air, or you can enlist a third party to supply practicality. Business should be imaginative, creative, charity.

Pisces with Aries

This can work quite well, especially at first. Pisces admires the dynamism of Aries, who often has the get-up-and-go when Pisces got-up-and-went. Aries relishes the support and admiration of the Fish, who rarely, if ever, challenges the Ram's ego and leadership.

As lovers   This can be very passionate. Both of these signs are idealistic, both dream of the perfect love and both seek extremes of experience. Ms Pisces feels that now she has met her knight in shining armour, just when it seemed life was a rust-bucket that left her alone with her fantasies. Mr Pisces is inspired to poetry by his heroine. Piscean appreciation is a great encouragement to Aries; however, Pisces may mistake all that bravado for real action (which it isn't always), and wake up to find that they are two lost children – only Aries won't admit it. Aries may wound Pisces with insensitivity and Aries may become enraged when Pisces can't/won't clarify his or her feelings. Aries needs to be just a little thoughtful and Pisces wise to make this work long term.

As friends   Pisces must be careful not to become a sacrifice to Arien needs and projects. Pisces must be sure of what he or she wants and make sure that Aries knows about it. Aries can certainly enliven Pisces' life, but Pisces must look elsewhere for emotional support.

As business partners   You are both likely to have lots of ideas and enthusiasm. Aries is impatient about getting going while Pisces is intuitive about people, and may find any hidden drawbacks. It is possible this partnership could lack 'finishiative', and so some Earthly input is desirable. You could make a million or be a damp squib, so think carefully about what you are doing.

Pisces with Taurus

There is much to recommend this partnership, for Taurus is synonymous with Earthy solidity and Pisces with fluidity, so Pisces can find a supportive 'container' in the Bull, while Taurus can find some imagination and adaptability in the Fish. At least that's how it *can* be, in the best of scenarios. In practice, Taurus can dismiss all Piscean dreams with a snort, and Piscean elusiveness can be like a red rag to the Bull who may then trample on everything with dogmatic statements and refusals. Taurus may be left to sit alone in the muddy wreckage.

As lovers   This can be wonderful, for Pisces responds to Taurean sensuality, encouraging a more-ish interchange. Ms Pisces feels that at last she has found a rock on which to bask, while Mr Pisces senses that here is a woman who can give form to some of his imagining and help him to greater effectuality. However, Taurus is extremely tactless at times, and while the Taurean presence may offer security, there is often little forthcoming in the way of the emotional support Pisces needs. After being told not to be 'stupid' once too often, Pisces may seek understanding elsewhere and Taurus can become mega-jealous. This may drive Pisces to a 'martyr-ish' stance (and, mysteriously, too ill to have sex), or it may mean that Pisces just goes absent. You two have much to offer each other and in many ways are just what the other needs, but you need to remind yourselves of this, regularly.

As friends   You could share aesthetic pursuits. Taurus is good at keeping Piscean feet on the ground, while Pisces encourages Taurus to lighten up. However, without sex there might be little to draw you together, and you may irritate each other.

As business partners   Pisces may be happy to let Taurus handle accounts and organisation, while providing the ideas. Could work well.

Pisces with Gemini

Both these signs are extremely changeable and may understand each other on that basis. However, Pisces' medium is the Watery one, of emotions, while Gemini is Airy and more cerebral. You may find considerable compatibility and then, all of a sudden, find yourselves stranded on opposite sides of a verbal stream ('*What* are you talking about?'). Gemini may talk of the difficulties of 'sensitive people'; Pisces isn't sure who Gemini means or wonders whether Gemini is being critical of Piscean emotionalism. Pisces reaches for the clear Air of Geminian thought while Gemini is fascinated by Pisces' Watery depths. You have much to offer each other, if you can only manage to benefit from it.

As lovers At first this can be enthralling. Ms Pisces finds Mr Gemini's wit and agile brain seductive while Mr Pisces is charmed by the mercurial Ms Gemini. However, Pisces may wonder what is happening when Gemini words are not backed up by deeds, and the relationship could turn into one of shadow boxing, misunderstanding and absences, with Pisces complaining and Gemini becoming sarcastic. However, this relationship can also be exciting, compelling and possess an indefinable 'something'. Gemini must accept that there are some things the mind cannot encompass, and that Pisces and this relationship are two of them. Pisces must appreciate that the inspiring Geminian mental qualities of versatility and perception would be dulled by too much emotion and not to try to 'kill the thing they love'.

As friends Lots of chatter. There are some things Pisces won't tell Gemini, and Gemini may find Pisces 'moody'.

As business partners Gemini thinks, Pisces feels – who will do the deeds? A third party may be needed for stability.

Pisces with Cancer

These two get along beautifully, for there is so much rapport. Cancer may be protective towards Pisces, while Pisces responds with infinitive understanding and attempts to beguile Cancer from the worst of his or her fears. Being quite similar, they may get each other down, sinking into a moody morass. Pisces is more 'cosmic' in consciousness than Cancer, and it is possible that Cancer may find this a threat, while Pisces may feel suffocated by Cancerian parochialism. However, understanding and sympathy usually prevail.

As lovers   The sexual relationship can be quite sublime; here we have 'such things as dreams are made on'. Ms Pisces feels safe with Mr Cancer, who seems to understand all her fears and needs, while Mr Pisces enjoys being 'mothered' just a little by a woman who is as feminine as she is circumspect. One problem is that this could become a 'gruesome twosome' with each feeding the other's fears, until it's 'you and me against the world'. Cancer may feel uneasy when Pisces is 'spaced out', and at such times closeness could be ruptured leaving each cold and lonely. However, for the most part this is an ideal couple.

As friends   Lots of giggles and gossip. Both of you sees deeply into the human heart and intimate details are your currency. Cancer is good at talking sense into Pisces, because of coming from a position of understanding, while Pisces can open up Cancerian perspectives.

As business partners   This can work, because Cancer is usually careful with money and both have terrific imagination. However, if you both become a prey to fears your venture will lack dynamism. Cancer may find Pisces rather unambitious and unrealistic, but then so do most people.

Pisces with Leo

Leonine warmth and fearless egocentricity can be a real tonic to Pisces, or may make her or him shrink and run a mile. The Lion often reacts well to Piscean admiration and responsiveness and may be protective and encouraging, while Piscean faith in life expands and blossoms. However, if Leo is too overbearing Pisces is likely to slip away, leaving the Lion affronted and bewildered – and nasty to come home to!

As lovers Passionate and romantic, especially at first. The strong feelings of Leo are a great turn-on to sybaritic Pisces, who knows just how to fan the Leonine flame until it glows. Leo, in turn, gives Pisces the conviction that all dreams are possibilities. Ms Pisces is wrapt by this larger-than-life character, while Mr Pisces finds Ms Leo dazzling. However, Leo can be bossy and there is only so much of this that Pisces can take, although there are some accommodating Pisceans, and these will eventually irritate the Lion irrationally, because of the sneaking feeling they are dominating a vacuum. In addition, Pisces is unreliable at times, and that will not do for possessive Leo, who may be driven to extremes by Piscean elusiveness. Also the Piscean reluctance to explain or to say what he or she wants can be exasperating to Leo, while Pisces can find Leo invasive. For this to work Pisces needs to learn to be more upfront and Leo needs to acquire tolerance and lots of imagination.

As friends There could be lots of fun in this friendship and you may share interests in drama, music and similar, for you stimulate each other's love of life. Pisces must be firm, Leo must bite his or her tongue.

As business partners Big on ideas, small on practicality, here is where Pisces is *too* supportive. Get some down-to-earth input.

Pisces with Virgo

A real meeting of the particular with the general. Here we have zodiacal opposites, which means you can balance each other or run each other ragged. A more chaotic Pisces will pitch Virgo into the obsessive-compulsive, while Virgoan fussing will drive Pisces to seek any form of escape. However, there is an orderly side to many Pisceans, who will appreciate the methodical Virgoan approach, while Virgo can be secretly mesmerised by the 'Cosmic Cod'.

As lovers   In the presence of dreamy, accepting Pisces, Virgo can become relaxed and sensual. The Earthy Virgoan can be arousing to Pisces, and provided neither partner is too fastidious or idealistic, sex can be good. Ms Pisces feels reassured by a man who seems to know how to take care of all those boring details, and Mr Pisces feels rather similar about Ms Virgo, admiring everything from the nettle soup to the sheer black nylons. However, Virgo is a Mutable sign, and may not be able to provide the security Pisces needs. Pisces may feel there is always something wrong, and life may be a contest regarding who can worry most intensively, about the most things. Pisces needs to remember that there is a security that rests in Virgo's practical, detailed approach, but that Virgo is fine soil rather than hard rock. Give each other space – you can achieve a lot if you have confidence in each other.

As friends   Sometimes this works well if you have a shared goal, but Pisces may be irritated and undermined by Virgo and will seize up or disappear, or become waspish, if criticised. You share a sensitive and adaptable approach; for the rest say '*Vive la difference*'.

As business partners   A Pandora's box of worries, with Hope trapped under the lid. Virgo could feel threatened, Pisces shredded. A third party is needed to appreciate both, mediate and decide.

Pisces with Libra

This can be an aesthetic, gentle and lovely partnership because both partners are tactful and intent on pleasing. The trouble is, no one wants to make the decisions. It is quite possible that Libra could be forced into doing this and feeling perpetually uneasy about it. As a couple you may miss trains and boats and planes with regularity.

As lovers Attraction between Air and Water can be strong and there is likely to be a significant amount of fantasy and ritual, to which both partners are drawn. Ms Pisces delights in the *savoir-faire* of Libra, while Mr Pisces admires the intelligence and femininity of Ms Libra. Both of you are idealistic, but the ideals, although superficially similar, may be poles apart underneath. Pisces may eventually feel stranded by the fact that Libra seems so intent on the image of the partnership, yet seems so unwilling to be carried away by real emotion. Libra, through diplomacy, can encourage Pisces to find some detachment, while Pisces can add depth to Libra and present her or him with an unfathomable mystery, which further enhances Libra's fascination with the partnership as a whole – but this needs work.

As friends You may enjoy much in each other's company, if you have the same tastes, for you can wax lyrical together. You may each feel the other has a valuable secret; however, the problem with the two of you, as always, could be getting off your butts, and you may toy with ideas endlessly until you find the party's over.

As business partners Not to be recommended, for you are both extravagant and all too easily distracted by window dressing. Also, neither of you is typically a grafter. You will need some input from Earth or Fire, and all your native charm, to get by.

Pisces with Scorpio

No one understands the Scorpion quite like Pisces – except perhaps another Scorpio, and then there may be competition. Pisces is usually accepting, understanding and wise enough to know how Scorpio feels, and Scorpio is often protective and strengthening towards Pisces. This can be a relationship of great depth and intensity.

As lovers   Extremely passionate and emotional. Both partners see sex as a passage to the transcendent and the highs may be tremendous. Scopionic intensity can make Pisces feel reassured, while Piscean responsiveness if just what Scorpio yearns for without letting on in words. Ms Pisces is excited by this strong and secret character, while Mr Pisces finds the charisma of Ms Scorpio irresistible. The main problem this relationship may run into is that Pisces is elusive, and Scorpio is possessive. Pisces finds it hard at times to say what he or she means and almost impossible to give chapter and verse about every area of the Fish's life. Pisces may forgive Scorpio if the Scorpion is caught going through the Fish's pockets, but Pisces may take up a long-suffering stance and a lot of inter-manipulation can ensue. Don't waste your energies in this way. Look into each other's eyes and you will know the truth.

As friends   Lots of empathy and rapport, you can enjoy doing anything together because you are greatly in harmony. Pisces rarely provokes the Scorpion's 'sting' although Scorpio may become impatient at times with Pisces. However, if the relationship is sufficiently close, Scorpio realises that Piscean sensitivity is not the same as weakness, and admires the subtle strength. Mutually supportive.

As business partners   Scorpio is tough and good with money. Each values the other's imagination. Could work well.

Pisces with Sagittarius

These two may have certain things in common, for the original ruler of Pisces was Jupiter, shared with Sagittarius. There is a shared love of life, *bonhomie* and philosophy, and there may be a gipsy in the soul of each – and there's the rub! Neither of you is that reliable. Pisces may feel continually let down and insecure with Sagittarius, while Sagittarius may be irrationally put out when she or he eventually wanders home to an empty house.

As lovers   Extremely romantic at first, with a sizeable fantasy element. Pisces feels encouraged by Sagittarius, while the Archer believes that Pisces can fulfil all his or her ideals and ask little in return. Ms Pisces may feel that Mr Sagittarius can accomplish anything, while Mr Pisces is impressed by the energy and enterprise of Ms Sagittarius. After a while Pisces may feel that there is a lot of hot air and little substance. Sagittarius may feel that Pisces is not up-front enough. Pisces can feel trampled, Sagittarius betrayed. This partnership is helped by a strong dose of realism, by each partner being careful to say what he or she means, by Sagittarius counting to ten before the horse's mouth opens, and by Pisces looking elsewhere for emotional rapport. Nurture your shared dreams.

As friends   There may be much to share in the way of discussion about beliefs and experiences. If you share a similar philosophy you may find that you stimulate each other and that life seems interesting when you are together. The problem may be that Sagittarius isn't there when Pisces needs her or him, and Sagittarius may find it hard to understand Pisces.

As business partners   Bad news here, I'm afraid. You are liable to encourage each other to go to ever greater extremes, until all sense of realism is lost. You may have some great ideas – get sound advice.

Pisces with Capricorn

Possibly the best Earth sign for the Fish, Capricorn offers stability and while not always a whizz at emotional rapport and support, Capricorn is always there and tends to offer practical support, while being unflappable and realistic about Piscean anxieties.

As lovers   Pisces is well able to coax out the orgiastic aspect of the Goat, and the sexual side is likely to be good. Pisces may wonder why Capricorn always puts work first, but may come to appreciate this when the bills get paid. Ms Pisces feels 'rescued' by Capricorn, who is the original strong and silent type for her to lean on. Mr Pisces feels reassured by this capable and subtly sensual lady. As the last of the Earth signs there is often a side to Capricorn that is unexpectedly open to hidden realms, although the Goat rarely gets carried away. Pisces can answer something in the questing side of Capricorn, while Pisces is rendered more effectual and sensible by being brought firmly down to earth once in a while. The only drawback to this duo can be found with the more dour type of Capricorn, who kills Piscean dreams, or the more fluffy Pisces, whom Capricorn can't be doing with.

As friends   This may be an enduring friendship. As 'Cardinal Earth' Capricorn lacks the stodginess of Taurus and the nervous quality of Virgo. Pisces may be continually encouraged by the practical, active nature of Capricorn, who is often interested by Piscean schemes. Pisces paints the verbal picture, Capricorn gets out the map. Pisces dreams while Capricorn sends for the brochure.

As business partners   This has much to recommend it, because Pisces may have some great ideas and Capricorn can put them into practice, with dotted i's and crossed t's. Daring and confidence may be lacking.

Pisces with Aquarius

These two are often drawn together, because they are both idealistic, and all things can seem possible at first. However, the cerebral and detached nature of Aquarius means that the emotional rapport that Pisces needs is perpetually lacking, and Aquarius can feel tied down and mystified by Pisces, endlessly trying to rationalise.

As lovers Initially, fascination can be intense. Pisces can feel turned on by an unreachable something in Aquarius, and Aquarian reactions are similar, for Pisces is one sign who tends to defy analysis. Ms Pisces may be temporarily enslaved by this remote character, while Mr Pisces finds the friendliness and careless charm of Aquarius magnetic. However, the Aquarian obsession with freedom can be hurtful to Pisces. Pisces may be aware of emotional undercurrents and unable to understand why Aquarius persists in denying his or her feelings. Aquarius is sincere, and cannot understand why Pisces behaves the way he or she does. In the long run, both may be hurt, and Aquarius, having given his or her heart for life is bewildered. Pisces can leave a piece of her or his own heart behind and seek somewhere warmer. For this to work Pisces must acquire detachment and learn to appreciate that Aquarius does offer security – of a kind and Aquarius needs to admit to being troubled and confused by emotional feelings.

As friends There may be lots of shared interests, and with no emotional expectations this could be interesting and stimulating. Pisces must forgive Aquarian brusqueness and value the inspiring qualities. Aquarius must not try to sort out Pisces.

As business partners Rather unpredictable. Could be too whacky for success. Aquarius is often good with the purse strings, while Pisces can handle PR and have a 'feel' for the market trends. Something 'fringe' that doesn't need a lot of investment could work.

Appendix 3

■ TRADITIONAL ASSOCIATIONS AND TOTEM

Each sign of the zodiac is said to have an affinity with certain colours, plants, stones and other substances. Of course, we cannot be definite about this, for not only do sources vary regarding specific correspondences – we also have the rest of the astrological chart to bear in mind. Some people also believe that the whole concept of such associations is invalid. However, there certainly do seem to be some links between the character of each of the signs and the properties of certain substances. It is up to you to experiment and to see what works for you.

Anything that traditionally links with Pisces is liable to intensify Piscean traits. So if you wish for some reason to be practical or self-assertive, then steer clear of the colours blue and green, and ylang-ylang essential oil! However, if you want to be your Piscean, dreamy best, it may help to surround yourself with the correct stimuli, especially on a down day. Here are some suggestions:

- **Colours**   Shades of blue, green, violet or purple. Sometimes wine, silver.
- **Flowers**   Gardenia, honeysuckle, jasmine, mimosa, sweet pea.
- **Metal**   Pewter, also silver.
- **Stones**   Amethyst, sugilite, mother-of-pearl, turquoise.

Aromatherapy

Aromatherapy uses the healing power of essential oils both to prevent ill health and to maintain good health. Specific oils can sometimes be used to treat specific ailments. Essential oils are concentrated and powerful substances, and should be treated with respect. Buy from a reputable source. *Do not use any oil in pregnancy* until you have checked with a reputable source that it is okay. *Do not ingest oils* – they act through the subtle medium of smell, and are absorbed in massage. *Do not place undiluted on the skin.* For massage: Dilute in a carrier oil such as sweet almond or grapeseed, two drops of oil to one teaspoon of carrier. Use in an oil burner, six to ten drops at a time, to fragrance your living area.

Essential oils

- **Ylang-ylang** Good for aiding recovery from shock, frustration and for regulating the heartbeat. Generally soothing, langourous and sensuous. Also soothes discordant and painful emotions, such as jealousy.
- **Eucalyptus** Helpful for relieving catarrh and respiratory problems, flu and colds. Generally healing, purifying and protecting.
- **Clove** Sharp and spicy, this oil is associated with Pisces through its original ruler, Jupiter. It is a good antiseptic and helps digestive infections. A drop applied direct to a troublesome tooth can take away toothache.
- **Jasmine** Exquisite, and expensive! It encourages optimism and confidence, being both relaxing and fortifying. Helpful for nervous debility, in childbirth, menstrual cramps and post-natal depression. Beneficial to inflamed skin.

Naturally you are not restricted to oils ruled by your sign, for in many cases treatment with other oils will be beneficial, and you should consult a reputable source (see 'Further Reading') for advice if you have a particular problem. If a problem persists, consult your GP.

Your birth totem

According to the tradition of certain native North American tribes, each of the signs of the zodiac is known by a totem animal. The idea of the totem animal is useful, for animals are powerful, living symbols and they can do much to put us in touch with our potentials. Knowing your totem animal is different from knowing your sign, for your sign is used to define and describe you – as we have been doing in this book – whereas your totem shows you a path of potential learning and growth.

The totem for Pisces is the Wolf, and you also have an affinity with Buffalo and Frog. You were born in the Blustery Winds Time. The North American lore is based on the seasonal cycle, thus for those of you in the Southern Hemisphere, it may be worth bearing in mind the totems for your opposite sign, Virgo. These are Brown Bear, also Mouse and possibly Turtle, though Turtle is for the Earth clan and the Virgoan time is Harvesting Time.

Wolf has much to offer Pisces, for Wolf is a teacher and a pathfinder, with great physical strength and stamina and an uncanny ability to smell and track. These are gentle animals, with a strong sense of pack, only vicious when forced to be so. Wolf shows a fierce and tenacious side to Pisces, and as a 'walker between the worlds' Wolf can show the trails of the spirits.

Contacting your totem

You can use visualisation techniques to make contact with the energies of your birth totem. You will need to be very quiet, still and relaxed. Make sure you won't be disturbed. Have a picture of your birth totem before you, and perhaps burn one of the essential oils we have mentioned, in an oil burner, to intensify the atmosphere.

When you are ready close your eyes and imagine that you are your totem animal. Imagine how it feels, what it sees, smells, hears. What are its feelings, instincts and abilities? Keep this up for as long as you are comfortable, then come back to everyday awareness. Write down your experiences and eat or drink something to ground you. This can be a wonderfully refreshing and mind-clearing exercise, and you may find it inspiring. Naturally, if you feel you have other totem animals – creatures with which you feel an affinity – you are welcome to visualise those. Look out for your totems in the wild – there may be a message there for you.

Further reading
and resources

Astrology for Lovers, Liz Greene, Unwin, 1986. The title may be misleading, for this is a serious, yet entertaining and wickedly accurate account of the signs. A table is included to help you find your Rising Sign. This book is highly recommended.

Teach Yourself Astrology, Jeff Mayo and Christine Ramsdale, Hodder & Stoughton, 1996. A classic textbook for both beginner and practising astrologer, giving a fresh insight to birth charts through a unique system of personality interpretation.

Love Signs for Beginners, Kristyna Arcarti, Hodder & Stoughton, 1995. A practical introduction to the astrology of romantic relationships, explaining the different roles played by each of the planets and focussing particularly on the position of the Moon at the time of birth.

Star Signs for Beginners, Kristyna Arcarti, Hodder & Stoughton, 1993. An analysis of each of the star signs – a handy, quick reference.

The Moon and You for Beginners, Teresa Moorey, Hodder & Stoughton, 1996. Discover how the phase of the Moon when you were born affects your personality. This book looks at the nine lunar types – how they live, love, work and play, and provides simple tables to enable you to find out your birth phase and which type you are.

The New Compleat Astrologer, Derek and Julia Parker, Mitchell Beazley, 1984. This is a complete introduction to astrology with instructions on chart calculation and planetary tables, as well as clear and interesting descriptions of planets and signs. Including history and reviewing present-day astrology, this is an extensive work, in glossy, hardback form, with colour illustrations.

The Knot of Time: Astrology and the Female Experience, Lindsay River and Sally Gillespie. For personal growth, from a gently feminine perspective, this book has much wisdom.

The Astrology of Self-discovery, Tracy Marks, CRCS Publications, 1985. This book is especially useful for Moon signs.

The Astrologer's Handbook, Francis Sakoian and Louis Acker, Penguin, 1984. This book explains chart calculation and takes the reader through the meanings of signs and planets, with extensive interpretations of planets in signs and houses. In addition, all the major aspects between planets and angles are interpreted individually. A very useful work.[a]

Aromatherapy for Pregnancy and Childbirth, Margaret Fawcett RGN, RM, LLSA, Element, 1993.

The Aromatherapy Handbook, Daniel Ryman, C W Daniel, 1990.

Useful addresses

The Faculty of Astrological Studies
The claim of the Faculty to provide the 'finest and most comprehensive astrological tuition in the world' is well founded. Correspondence courses of a high calibre are offered, leading to the internationally recognised diploma. Evening classes, seminars and summer schools are taught, catering for the complete beginner to the most experienced astrologer. A list of trained consultants can be supplied on request, if you wish for a chart interpretation. For further details telephone (UK code) 0171 700 3556 (24-hour answering service); or fax 0171 700 6479. Alternatively, you can write, with SAE, to: Ref. T. Moorey, FAS., BM7470, London WC1N 3XX, UK.

Educational

California Institute of Integral Studies, 765 Ashbury St, San Francisco, CA 94117. Tel: (415) 753-6100

Kepler College of Astrological Arts and Sciences, 4518 University Way, NE, Suite 213, Seattle, WA 98105. Tel: (206) 633-4907

Robin Armstrong School of Astrology, Box 5265, Station 'A', Toronto, Ontario, M5W 1N5, Canada. Tel: (416) 923-7827

Vancouver Astrology School, Astraea Astrology, Suite 412, 2150 W Broadway, Vancouver, V6K 4L9, Canada. Tel: (604) 536-3880

The Southern Cross Academy of Astrology, PO Box 781147, Sandton, SA 2146 (South Africa) Tel: 11-468-1157; Fax: 11-468-1522

Periodicals

American Astrology Magazine, PO Box 140713, Staten Island, NY 10314-0713. e-mail: am.astrology@genie.gies,com

The Journal of the Seasons, PO Box 5266, Wellesley St, Auckland 1, New Zealand. Tel/fax: (0)9-410-8416

The Federation of Australian Astrologers Bulletin, PO Box 159, Stepney, SA 5069. Tel/fax: 8-331-3057

Aspects, PO Box 2968, Rivonia 2128, SA (South Africa)
Tel: 11-864-1436

Realta, The Journal of the Irish Astrological Association, 4 Quay Street, Galway, Ireland. Available from IAA, 193, Lwr Rathmines Rd, Dublin 6, Ireland.

Astrological Association, 396 Caledonian Road, London, N1 1DN. Tel: (UK code) 0171 700 3746; Fax: 0171 700 6479. Bi-monthly journal issued.